WHAT HAPPENS IN PSYCHOANALYSIS is divided into three sections. Each corresponds to a particular stage in psychoanalysis. The first deals with that phase of therapy called positive transference, the second with negative transference, and the third with the period of increasing psychic health. For everyone who needs, wants, or plans treatment, this book offers the immense advantage of knowing what to expect.

Lucy Freeman, a New Yorker, was educated at Bennington College. She has been a **New York Times** reporter as well as a successful writer and lecturer.

Other Books by the Same Author

FIGHT AGAINST FEARS

HOPE FOR THE TROUBLED

BEFORE I KILL MORE

HOSPITAL IN ACTION: The Story of the Michael Reese Medical Center

SEARCH FOR LOVE

What Happens in Psychoanalysis

(Original title: So You Want to Be Psychoanalyzed!)

Lucy Freeman

McGraw-Hill Book Company

New York Toronto London

Library of Congress Catalog Card Number: 58-7638

Published by arrangement with
HOLT, RINEHART & WINSTON, INC.

345678910 MUMU 76543210

Printed in the United States of America

Preface

This is fantasy.

No analysis ever happened quite like this. No analyst, no man or woman on the couch, ever spoke quite these words or shared these fragments. Yet they hold, in some measure, a part of every analysis.

Any flippancy, exaggeration, or irony should be forgiven since it is all done in good humor except for the rare remarks that stem from unconscious rage for which, of course, the author accepts no responsibility.

L. F.

Prologue

Once upon a twentieth-century time atom bombs and hydrogen bombs and earth satellites and rockets to outer space exploded in the world.

But there also came into the world a way for man to look within himself.

Thus he could decide whether to use the atom bombs and hydrogen bombs and earth satellites and rockets to outer space for evil or good.

Contents

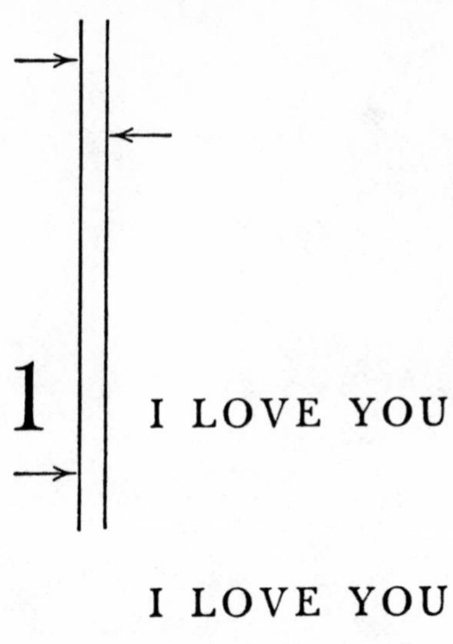

I LOVE YOU

I LOVE YOU

Inward, Ho!

There you are, at long last, all the reasons why you avoided psychoanalysis finally overridden.

Years of postponement, fear of being thought crazy or of wasting time and money—the excuses lie in limbo.

You are now stretched out on the couch, staring at the ceiling while behind you sits a shadowy figure, listening, waiting for you to speak.

You fumble for a handkerchief and blow your nose tremulously. You sniff several times in sorrow for yourself and the wretched world. You clear your parched throat.

Then you ask, "What am I supposed to say?"

"Anything that comes to mind," replies the figure behind you.

"What's the purpose?" you ask.

"That is how you reach your unconscious," he explains.

"I'm not sure I want to," you mutter.

"That's what you are here for," he says patiently.

"Oh!" you exclaim at this revolutionary idea. "How will I know when I reach my unconscious?"

"That is not your concern," he says.

That means it is *his* concern, and you are delighted that something is, because maybe then he will talk to you once in a while. You have heard that analysts are psychically strong, silent types.

He certainly does not intend to begin in Demosthenic fashion, for he now retreats into a cocoon of silence. Under other circumstances you could fight silence with silence; but to lie here in frightened, rebellious muteness would be cutting off your voice to spite your psyche.

With a nervous laugh meant to put yourself at ease but which only makes you feel less than a cretin, you say, "I'm probably wasting your time. My life is really uncomplicated. Maybe I drink too much once in a while or take things a little too seriously but, heh—heh—that's par for the course, isn't it?"

Only silence rewards this halfhearted jest.

"Are you there?" you ask cheerfully. You want to make sure he has not dropped dead or is taking forty winks at a dollar-a-wink expense to you.

"Why would you think I wouldn't be?" he says.

"I—I don't know," you explain lamely. "You didn't say anything."

"I will. When I have something to say," he replies, and this is the thought that must sustain you for months to come in moments of darkest despair, when you feel if he does not say something, *anything,* you will rise zombie-like from the couch and do something desperate.

For nothing, absolutely nothing, carries the assaultive power of silence. Someone wrote that the first man to hurl a word of abuse instead of a spear started civilization. To this you would add that the man who then refused to hurl back a word of abuse but instead stood in silence furthered civilization by hundreds of years.

After what seems to you like ten minutes he asks, "What are you thinking about?"

At that very moment you are struck witless. Your mind is the perfect blank, giving the lie to science, which claims that this is not possible.

"There is nothing on my mind," you assure him. "My life has been a simple one, as I told you."

You are thinking that you have been a fool to believe otherwise, that you have everything you want, and that you have made a dreadful mistake in seeking help from this stranger.

"Do you really think it has been simple?" he asks.

You shrug your shoulders, say nothing.

"Is there anything troubling you at this point?" he asks.

Encouraged by this display of deep interest, you think that as long as he would like to know what is on your mind, you will tell him, idiotic though it be.

You start off: "It's silly but I stewed for hours last night wondering if I should visit the Smiths for a restful week end in the country. Restful–hah! Try resting when you are exiled to a bed that is a relic of the Ice Age. Or blasted into dawn by the taunting screams of little monsters. Or must pretend you do not see the angry glances exchanged between host and hostess over the trivial but deadly important trials of daily living. And then find yourself going to work Monday feeling you spent the week end in an emotional strait jacket."

"If you don't want to go, why go?" he asks in a kindly voice and you almost sit up with the shock. He cares enough to want to spare you torture? This is one of the few times in your life that another has shown such concern.

Although you want to thank him, you feel embarrassed and promptly think of reasons why you should endure the agonizing week end.

"It's hard to say no to a friend," you explain.

"You are apt to keep the friend longer if you feel free enough to say no at times," he says.

It never occurred to you that you did not have to visit the Smiths just because they asked, that their summons was not law.

"What are you thinking?" he asks unexpectedly.

"I—er—nothing," you reply hastily and he is understanding enough not to pursue the point.

Therefore you become bolder. "Why must I tell you everything I think? Why can't I choose what to say, like in ordinary conversation?"

"Because this is not ordinary conversation," he says.

"What kind of conversation is it?" you ask.

"It is no conversation at all," he says. "It is called 'free association' when *you* speak and 'interpretation' when *I* speak."

"My associations are not very free," you complain.

"You have just started," he says. "They will get freer. Just try not to censor what you say."

This is like telling you to stop breathing. But you manage to get out every third and fourth thought and hope he does not know that you are holding back. You cannot bring yourself to say some of the things that run through your mind, like you think he is charging too much and his taste in ties is atrocious and the painting on his wall would not do justice to a brothel.

When you first stumbled into the room you were not

conscious of anything in it but your trembling self and the formidable stranger. But gradually the room has taken shape and you have noticed the lank, naked lady in the painting on the wall.

You decide, since he asked for candor, to tell him what you think of the picture. You blurt out, "I don't like that," pointing to the nude.

"Does our taste in art have to be the same?" he says, not at all offended by your criticism.

"I guess not," you reply grudgingly, realizing there is no reason why you should have the same tastes in art or furnish your homes in the same period or choose the same people as friends.

At last those first fifty minutes end and you find yourself out of his office, wandering dazedly down the street and into the clamoring crowds. You feel somehow superior to mortal man who at this second is intent only on shoving you off the sidewalk in his rush to get nowhere.

You are prouder of yourself than ever before, prouder even than when you won the Phi Beta Kappa key. You, who considered yourself without the courage to break a chain letter, now dare to embark on a journey to the unknown faraway shores of your soul. You are game, no matter what the risk, to explore the psychic precipices, whirlpools, and volcanoes of your inner mind.

You have already forgotten the moment you walked into the analyst's office and he said hello in a quiet voice and you considered it a frontal attack on your integrity, even though you did not hear what he said and wondered, later, what it could have been. You shook as though reaching the final stages of delirium tremens. You stared in mute misery at the couch, turned to him with eyes that pleaded for a last-minute reprieve from this voyage into the dark land of repression.

You stood there wishing you were made of the stern stuff of those who plunged into enemy lines ahead of their troops and of those who would be the first to step upon the moon. But though you wanted to sling up your feet and fall back on the couch defiantly, mustering a wisecrack or two, such as, "Stop me if I snore," or, "Bring on the dancing girls," you could only stand paralyzed, all flippancy buried beneath fear.

Instead you muttered, "M—must I l-lie down?" frightened by a terrifying position that would reduce you to the ridiculous status of an infant in the crib, subject to anyone's attack.

"You don't have to," he said. "Do whatever is comfortable. It is just that lying down is the easiest way in the long run for both of us."

You would be delighted to do anything to make it easier in the long run for both. You lowered yourself to the couch as though onto a slab of spikes.

And now it is over and done. Trifling as it may appear in a cold-war world, you feel that a mighty battle has been won.

You wonder how you will endure the empty moments until the next meeting.

Anchors Away

The time for you to return for a second session finally arrives and you are back on the couch.

"I really don't know why I wanted to be analyzed," you say. "I guess I just got sick and tired of going to work each morning as though I were on my way to a rockpile."

Silence, so you go on. "I'm tired of taking peace pills and sleep pills and pep pills to get through the long days and even longer nights.'"

More silence. In a burst of confidence you admit, "The thought hit me one day, while I was rereading *Hamlet,* that I could not keep blaming the fast pace of city life or the shaky state of the world for my misfortunes, that in some strange fashion I was responsible for my fickle fate."

"It's not so fickle if you understand yourself," he says.

"I would like, by some miracle, to understand myself," you say eagerly. "I would like to feel in tune with the world instead of despising myself and the way I live, as the experience is laughingly called."

"Psychoanalysis is not miraculous," he says slowly.

"Oh, I'm not expecting a miracle," you assure him quickly. Then you ask, "But what is it?"

"You'll find out," he says.

Your family and friends have been only too eager to tell you what they think psychoanalysis is—strictly for the birds. Your reply to them is that the birds do not need it; they are far too emotionally healthy; you can tell that by the way they sing all the time.

You grant your family and friends that, naturally, they are eminently qualified to discuss the value of psychoanalysis. Who could be more so than one who has never had the least experience with it, who knows as much about psychoanalysis as he does about Sanskrit?

You inform the analyst, "I asked my best friend what he thought about psychoanalysis and he said I was crazy if I started, that I was as sane as anyone he knew.

"Then I asked him, 'Who do you know?' and we proceeded to judge the comparative sanity of mutual friends. One was drinking himself into literary oblivion after writing a successful first novel. Another, a stockbroker, was being eaten alive by ulcers. A third, in the advertising business, was set on breaking the record of slightly over one thousand affairs set by Don Juan."

You wait for an approving chuckle, which does not come, so you go on: "Our mutual friends did not appear destined for the life I desire, one that holds a fair measure of love and serenity. I would like the best that is, in this best and worst of all possible worlds."

Because he still says not a word, you decide to tell him what you hold against him. "The cost of analysis appalled me slightly until I added up the money I spent on vacations, new furniture, and unnecessary clothes. I guess I can afford it for a while."

You add facetiously, "I can always live on Spam and move to a wooden shack in the park."

You continue, "I worried, too, about the time it would take, four or five hours a week for the next two or three years. But I was honest with myself. I admitted there was nothing important I would be doing with those four or five hours a week."

You add ironically, "I could even throw away the entire next two or three years and never miss them if they are anything like the last ten or fifteen."

You think back over the past year of futility and how finally you furtively sought the name of a psychoanalyst. Disguising your voice, although you did not believe for a second you deceived him, you called your family doctor, whom you once heard praising psychoanalysis, asking him to recommend an analyst. You wrote the name on a piece of paper and every so often took it out of your pocket and stared at it, mesmerized.

One depressing day when headlines told of Russia's latest hostile move and of an unusually large number of vicious murders, you surreptitiously slipped the piece of paper, now worn almost to shreds, out of your pocket. You looked up the analyst's phone number, dialed it.

"Hello," said a feminine voice.

"Is the doctor there?" you whispered conspiratorially.

"Who shall I say is calling?" she wanted to know.

You hesitated, struck by the idea of giving a false name. But you decided at this very moment to fling away foolish fancy and gave your correct name complete with middle initial.

"Hello," said a low, rich, masculine voice.

"I'd like to make an appointment to see you," you said, voice quivering.

"Consultation or treatment?" he asked.

"Tre-treat—treatment," you stammered.

"Can you come in next Tuesday at ten?"

"A.M. or P.M.?" You knew this was a stupid question but you could not help asking, for you had to be sure of the hour.

There was silence, as if he were choking back a curse. But he replied courteously, "In the morning."

"I'll be there," you reassured him and hung up feeling you had started a long climb up a snowy mountain.

Every second between the moment you hung up and the moment you walked into his office, you had regretted making the call. You considered phoning him to break the appointment with the explanation, "I really didn't mean it. I was paying off an election bet." You hoped maybe you would be lucky enough before the week ended to fall ill with pneumonia or be struck by a hit-and-run driver.

When the very day descended on you, there was only one thing left to do. You told yourself that for years you belonged to the legion of the walking dead anyhow, and either you would come to life as a result of this tortured decision of yours or finish off the job of dying.

Suddenly you thought of a friend who was in his third year of analysis. You called, asked if he would meet you for lunch. He already had a luncheon date but deigned to spare you a few minutes for a drink.

After half a martini had warmed you into heroism, you asked in that casual manner which often masks the deepest desperation, "What happens to someone who goes into psychoanalysis?"

He stared at you with what you thought amused contempt. Then, seeming to take pity on your stricken look, and, perhaps, because you were paying for the drinks, he said, "No one can possibly tell another what happens in psychoanalysis," gulped down the rest of his martini and took off.

Now the analyst tells you that psychoanalysis is not a miracle, that you will have to find out for yourself what it is.

You sigh in despair. You repeat once again the theme song of the beginner in couch life, "What shall I talk about?"

"Anything that comes to mind," he replies once more, the theme song of the analyst to the beginner in couch life.

The thought strikes you that childhood is supposed to be the root of all misery, that unhappiness in later life arises from long-forgotten feelings.

"My childhood was an *extremely* happy one," you announce.

"Tell me about it," he says.

And your psychoanalysis, miracle or no, has started.

How Not to Win an Analyst

You have survived several sessions and one bright day you decide to help the analyst along by really finding out what psychoanalysis is all about.

You lug home technical tomes from the library, stay up late to read how psychoanalysis was born of the brains and heart of a man with the courage to face his secret self.

You read Freud's clinical cases as well as stuff like *The Psychopathology of Everyday Life* and *The Interpretation of Dreams,* books whose theories have helped change the destiny of thousands of unhappy lives.

Particularly you are interested in why you must lie down, and you find out that originally the couch was a hang-over from hypnosis, the method first used by Freud. As he began psychoanalysis proper, Freud felt that the prone position offered more relaxation once the patient lost fear of it. The analyst, too, you conclude, is able to think more freely if the patient is not watching him like a hawk, misinterpreting his every expression and gesture.

You memorize the definitions of important words such as "sublimation," "repression," "infantilism." You are eager to show the analyst how much of a head start you have on the whole business.

You begin, in your next session, by informing him in a most offhand way that you have just finished reading the second volume of Ernest Jones' life of Freud. You say, in a tone implying that he no doubt missed this point completely, "Jones believed Freud was the man destined to discover psychoanalysis because, in addition to sensitivity, brilliance, patience, and determination to seek the truth, Freud also was willing to believe in the improbable, unexpected, and incredible."

Then you add, wanting to bring the analyst into the discussion, "Nothing important has been added since Freud, don't you agree?"

He is silent for a moment and you are glad he is giving this vital question such careful consideration. He finally speaks. He says, "If you want a course in the theory of psychoanalysis, why don't you take one at a university? It's lots cheaper."

You are stunned. Instead of praising you for your perspicacity, he is damning you as didactic. This cruel blow, dooming to wasteland the many hours you spent boning up on psychoanalysis, halts you from spouting theory for at least eight minutes.

Your feelings are hurt but courageously you plunge into a personal problem—you bring up your desire to overeat, explaining, "Freud would call this an oral—"

The analyst interrupts with a sigh, "I wish you'd read Mother Goose instead of Freud."

"I don't understand." You wonder if his mind has

snapped under the strain of too many patients like yourself.

"You will someday," he says, settling back into silence.

There is something in you that craves definition of the big words, as if knowing what they mean will help you to understand yourself. Eventually you realize that discussing the meaning of words does not help you understand anything about yourself except that you want to discuss what words mean.

Expounding theories about analysis obstructs and delays reaching your unconscious which, God knows and you know too, is hard enough to do. The aim of analysis is not to instruct you in its underlying principles but to acquaint you with your unconscious; the two aims are completely, thoroughly, and irrevocably incompatible.

You recall what Louis Armstrong answered when someone demanded, "Define jazz so I can understand it." Replied the wise Louis, "If you got to have it defined, man, you ain't never goin' to understand it."

The analyst gives you the feeling that he realizes you probably know far more about psychoanalytic theory than he but, if you do not mind, strictly for your own sake, he would like you to follow this one suggestion—Say whatever comes to you in free-flowing fashion instead of concentrating on impressing him with your erudition and psychoanalytic insight.

But you are not going to give up easily. Your ability to intellectualize has always been dear to you. "I suppose this intellectualizing in which I occasionally indulge is known in the profession as a 'defense,' " you say defensively. You know from your extensive reading that anything, even sex, may be a defense if used in exaggerated or distorted form.

Upset by his attack on this cherished defense, you continue blindly, "I'm only being considerate of you. Suppose a patient refused to discuss theory or give interpretations, believing it was your prerogative and duty, not his. Why, you'd drop dead of the shock."

"I'd be happy to take the risk," he says drily.

You decide to get even by substituting the defense of wit for that of intellectualization. You lie in silence, plotting, preparing to toss off your own definitions. You say to him breezily, "Since you won't discuss the meaning of the big words with me, I've thought up my own definitions. Want to hear them?"

He is silent and you construe this as assent, which, of course, it is not. It is despair.

You begin, "For 'regression,' my definition is: The art of not acting your age."

You hope this brings a smile and, though you are tempted to turn around and find out, you remain face forward. You go on: "For 'projection,' I submit: The art of blaming others."

You chuckle to yourself as you think of the perfect example of projection you read about that morning in the newspaper. Police Lieutenant C. J. Denkman was driving slowly along the streets of Memphis in his police car. Suddenly a motorist sped across his path, stopped dead in front of him with a screech of brakes, and stepped out of the car. Walking over to the policeman and exhaling a blast of alcoholic fumes into his face, the motorist announced, "I arrest you for speeding and reckless driving." The police lieutenant took the hint and promptly arrested the young man for speeding and drunken driving. You marvel at how the motorist's psychic apparatus, as well as his automobile, was functioning at high speed as he projected onto the policeman his own wrongdoing.

You wonder whether to tell the analyst this story, then decide not to, as long as he did not laugh at your definitions. Instead you proceed with the definitions, by now a matter of honor.

"For 'rationalization,' I would say: The art of lying so unsuccessfully that you fool no one, *except* yourself."

"Do you have more?" he asks and his voice sounds slightly bitter.

"Just one," you reply courteously. "It wouldn't be a fit list without 'sublimation,' would it?"

You listen for a sound, even a sigh, but there is none and you mark this down as one of the fifty thousand or so rhetorical questions you will ask within the next months. You offer, " 'Sublimation': The art of not doing what you really feel like doing, so the world's work gets done."

"What did you dream last night?" he asks.

"Oh, just some crazy dream," you say, dismissing it.

No Tea Party, This

You sit in the outer office, waiting, for he is late. Nervously you pick up a very old *New Yorker*. You skim through the cartoons, not laughing at the one portraying a psychoanalyst saying to a man on a couch, "The trouble with you is that you *are* inferior."

You read Audax Minor to see if he picked the winner of a race by now a ghost of the far past. Your mind is only paying token attention to the words.

You hurl the magazine down, light a cigarette, take a few puffs, then crush it out angrily against the ashtray. You wonder what can be keeping him, whether he started the day late, or a patient was tardy, or he is giving extra time to the person before you. You stand up, look out the window, decide that maybe the thing to do would be to leave quickly, for obviously he does not want to see you or he would not keep you waiting.

By now he is fifteen minutes late. You catapult yourself

into a chair, demanding loudly of the empty room, "What in hell is the son-of-a-bitch doing?"

Three minutes later you walk into the room with the view from the couch and smile at him with the falsest of cheer.

"I'm sorry I was late," he apologizes.

"That's perfectly all right," you say as though you had not given the delay even a first thought. "I caught up with a *New Yorker* I had missed."

"You have a right to feel angry," he says.

"I'm *not* angry," you insist, turning purple with rage. "You must have good reason for being late. It's none of my business why you were late."

You feel, of course, it is very much your business, but you would die under torture rather than admit it. You wait for him to explain. He merely says, "If you are angry, say so."

Now you are struck with wonder. Someone is encouraging you to be angry with him! All your life you have been punished when you dared to show anger, and you are no longer able to bear it as anything but a flash of feeling that you quickly put away.

"You're not serious?" you ask.

"Of course I am," he answers.

"Why should I be angry at you? You're trying to help me," you say magnanimously.

"I failed to be on time for an appointment with you," he says.

You cannot understand this. You hate people who lose their temper at you, for you feel this is the height of ugliness, and you also fear people will not like you if you explode at them. You say, "You'd hate me if I was angry."

"Why would I hate you for a natural feeling?" he asks.

The fact that anger is a natural feeling would never have occurred to you if you had the lifetime of Methuselah for contemplation.

"It's not polite to be angry at one's analyst," you say ruefully.

"Psychoanalysis is not a tea party," he retorts.

He is warning you that you are not spending your hard-earned dollars so that you can better carry on the small deceits and politenesses of the past, but that you are spending them in relentless pursuit of phantoms that remain chained inside of you by fear.

Perhaps psychoanalysis is not a tea party for him, you think grimly, but for you it is the tea party of tea parties, *à la* Wonderland, and you must avoid getting your head stuffed into the pot like the dozing Dormouse.

"I have always made a point of being very polite to everyone," you tell him.

"So I have observed," he says. "Don't you get tired of being so compliant all the time? What are you doing with your real feelings?"

"These *are* my real feelings," you insist.

"Nonsense," he says. "Nobody could take what you do without feeling some anger. What about the times you've told me you gave in to people although they were clearly wrong?"

"Most of them haven't the brains of a bonefish," you mutter.

"Then why don't you tell them, politely but firmly, when you think you are right?"

"Because I am a sniveling Uriah Heep who must apologize for living," you snarl in your first display of rage.

"Isn't anger preferable?" he asks.

"Is it?" You are astonished at what appears to be a heresy against one of society's most civilized canons.

"At least it's honest to be aware of your anger. If you cover up your inner feelings, you'll never know what you think about anything. You'll just keep turning the anger against yourself."

All at once you get a glimmer of yourself as a craven, cringing soul holding back fury and being slowly sucked to death in the maelstrom of your own sweetness. You ask, "Why can't I admit anger?"

"Probably for many reasons," he says, in, for him, a sudden spate of loquacity, "one of which is that it was dangerous for you as a child to show anger, fearing that your parents would hate you, strike you, turn you out, or maybe even kill you, for parents have been known to kill a child who infuriates them. So you became angry at yourself, having to put the feelings *some*place."

Yes, you realize, feelings do not disappear like smoke blown to the whim of the winds. Feelings of love, if rebuffed, need to fasten on something, and a stamp album or butterflies or clothes will do if you feel that human beings do not want you.

"But I don't want to be mad at you," you tell the analyst.

"Why not?" he says. "I am delighted when you can express anger."

You take a deep breath, then say, "Well, I *was* furious today when you kept me waiting. I felt like I wanted to kill somebody. I called you a son-of-a-bitch." It is a relief to confess this.

"Sometimes I cannot help being late," he says in a low voice.

"You're just like my father," you say, your fury turning from the analyst. "He would often keep me waiting an hour, never even apologizing when he showed up, and I never dared say a word although I was so mad I could cry."

"It wasn't very considerate of him, was it?" he says.

You again feel shock—the shock of realizing he is not going to explode at you. You are receiving no anger in return for your hatred, only the feeling you have a right to be angry. More surprising, he welcomes your anger.

He does not object if you rage at him or at your parents. You felt over the years you must not admit anger at them even were they to be severely unjust.

"I suppose I have hidden my anger at many things," you say.

"Are you thinking of anything in particular?" he asks.

"I remember once when I was eighteen and home from college, full of fresh, exciting theories. One evening at the dinner table I dared to defy my father as we discussed politics. I opposed his conservative viewpoint. He cracked me across the mouth and I fled from the room."

"Why didn't you slap him back?" asks the analyst.

"What?" you gasp. This is completely unexpected.

"Both he and you might have felt better."

"Strike my father?" You are aghast. "The Bible says 'Honor thy parent.' It doesn't say, 'Thou shalt slug thy father when he slugs you.' "

"But don't parents have to deserve the honor? Sometimes they deserve the anger."

Perhaps they occasionally do, you think. Perhaps you do not always have to choke back your rage. You may allow yourself to feel anger at those who seem unfair to you. They are not necessarily right. To deserve honor, people must earn it.

You begin to look at the way you have so easily buried your feelings over the years. You are able for the first time to do this because you dared to express the faintest of anger at the analyst.

As of the Strength of Ten

But, despite your advance, you are not willing to admit it yet.

You start off the next session by telling a joke about the two men who met on the street after one of them had spent twenty years alone in the wilderness.

Said the one who remained in the city, "You must have come up with some great new ideas with all that time to think."

Replied the other, "Perhaps so. I decided that life is like a fountain."

"What?" exclaimed the shocked city dweller. "Is that all you conceived?"

"Well—maybe life *isn't* like a fountain," said the other dubiously.

Instead of laughing, the analyst asks, "Do you feel that what is happening here is like twenty years in the wilderness with nothing achieved?"

"It is tortoise pace," you admit. "If I went any slower I'd go backward."

"You are going backward," he reminds you, "into your past. That's one reason it is so slow."

The pace with which you feel analysis proceeds in the beginning drives you into a psychological St. Vitus's dance. The word "patient" is the greatest misnomer in the world, for you possess not a patient nerve in your body.

"Why does it take so long?" you wail. "Can you tell me why it's so slow reaching the heart of psychic matter?"

"It's a little thing called 'resistance,' " he says, "one of the words, I notice, that you failed to define in jest." (He does not miss a trick!) "Resistance is probably the reason analysis is necessary at all. If we did not possess it, we would be able to know the unconscious effortlessly."

"And all be dead of shock at the age of ten, and overpopulation would be no problem," you remark sarcastically.

"Why did you pick the age of ten?" he asks.

"Just grabbed it out of the air," you say airily. Later you learn that nothing is just grabbed out of the air, that everything you say holds specific meaning in your life; but at this stage you are still naïve and full of resistance.

Your resistance is made up of a number of remarkably strong psychic legions known as defenses. You find out all too soon that the strength of one defense is as the strength of ten giants. Next to a defense, the Rock of Gibraltar is a shaky pillar of salt.

The most excruciating physical pain has nothing on how you suffer when your analyst smashes against your most treasured defenses, for you have spent years on the most desperate work of building them up. You burn with deepest anger, want to hit back.

You do not, of course, because if you have sense enough to be lying on his couch, you have sense enough to know he is trying to help you in his own ghastly way. You are dimly aware that it is your precious defenses that have made your life such a mess.

"How did I select my defenses?" you ask.

"As a child you chose whatever you felt offered you protection or got you attention, or you chose what you admired or envied or even what you despised," he says. "There's only one trouble with defenses."

"What's that?" you ask.

"They never work."

"Why not?"

"A defense is erected to hold back alien thoughts and feelings," he says. "But the defense does not mean the end of such thoughts and feelings. It is just the beginning. They reappear double-strength, wearing disguises that confuse you, that sometimes make you doubt your senses."

"Ah!" you exclaim triumphantly. "What Freud calls 'the return of the repressed.' "

"Yes," he says, wonder of wonders not castigating you for hauling out theory. "As long as you remain unaware of what you repress, you are haunted by it. The unconscious keeps hurling it back at you, again and again, to influence what you do."

It is like being an unwilling puppet on strings pulled by your unknown self, you think.

"How do I recognize a defense?" you ask.

"It's easy—in someone else," he says. "You cannot see your own without the help of an analyst; but just let another person show the same defense and you can see it clearly enough. It angers you, as a rule."

You can understand that if someone enrages you, what

you do not like about him is, often, what you do not like about yourself. You are prone to attack the one who acts as the mirror of your hidden self. The woman who loves to carry tales says disparagingly of another, "She's such a gossip," and the man who philanders is the first to accuse another of unfaithfulness.

"Why did I start building defenses?" you ask.

"You latched onto them when you were a child as protection against some deep hurt or fear or impulse. You have continued to clutch at them with the passion of a drowning person at a rotted plank."

"Defenses are my psychic Pyrrhic victories," you muse.

And in analysis they've got to go. Otherwise you cannot face the feelings they hide. "But the king is naked," cried the little boy who, alone, did not tremble in fear as did the adults who denied the king's nakedness, and you too can see the naked truth only if you are unafraid.

"In spite of my rebel resistance, can I be analyzed?" you ask fearfully, fearfully lest you can, fearfully lest you cannot.

"You're here, aren't you?" he says.

Much of his job consists of chipping off your defenses in the most delicate drop-of-water-wearing-away-rock style. He makes the same point over and over. Somewhere along the psychoanalytic way, after he has said a thing twenty or thirty times, you suddenly hear him and think, "Yes, what he's just said is true. I wonder why he never mentioned this before."

It is a mystery why analysts never kill patients. It can but be proof of their faith in man's ability to change plus the knowledge of how mightily he resists change.

You are not obtuse on purpose when you refuse to admit something the analyst says, because you know you are throwing away your money. You will only have to spend time on it later instead of going on to something else. It is just that, at the moment, what he says hurts too much. Your self-esteem is already shot full of as many holes as it can stand for the time being.

After a particularly profound session in which you are able to rip through a defense and glimpse feelings underneath, you sometimes feel beaten. You want only to stagger home and fall under the bedclothes, but somehow you pull together your shaken psyche and stumble on.

It is an exhaustion different from any you have known. It is not the exhaustion after eighteen holes of golf on a July day. Nor the exhaustion that follows psychological battles with your family, possibly the most strenuous form of exercise known to man.

It is an exhaustion that holds a sense of triumph.

Never Underestimate the Power of the Unconscious

"I'm so embarrassed," you confess. "I forgot an appointment yesterday, one I should have kept. I can't imagine what possessed me."

"Try imagining," he suggests.

"Why?" you ask.

"So you can find out the unconscious reason you did not want to keep that date."

You knew all the time you had such a hidden reason, but you just wanted to hear him say it. You are aware that the hour is nearly at hand when he will not explain it once more.

"What in blazes *is* my unconscious?" you suddenly ask.

He often makes strong distinction between what is unconscious and what is conscious and never the twain do meet in your feelings, although you have the uncomfortable idea he considers them inseparably intertwined.

"You'll find out for yourself," he says. "Let's start now. What about the date you forgot?"

"A friend wanted me to speak to my boss about getting her a job. I wasn't sure I could or should ask him."

"So, to avoid putting yourself and him on the spot, you forgot the date with her. Wouldn't it have been easier just to say no to your friend in the first place?"

"I suppose so," you say. "I wouldn't be feeling guilty now at having forgotten the appointment."

"Your unconscious tried to spare you the greater pain—of refusing her," he says.

"I'm not so sure of that," you mutter.

You become less sure of anything you have previously thought, as, slowly, hour by hour, week by week, month by month, in a way that permits no turning back, you start to know your unconscious, the part of you whose existence you somehow sense but cannot quite admit. It is the still, small voice within you which is often in danger of being lost in the urgent shuffle for survival. It contains the deepest recesses of memory, some of it so buried you will never reach it.

There is another part of you from which thoughts rise as you need them, like the date on which the battleship *Maine* was sunk or who said, "There but for the grace of God go I." If you went around with this kind of information always conscious, you would be cousin to the Univac. This knowledge you keep in your preconscious, which lies between your conscious and unconscious.

But from the unconscious you can summon little without the help of an analyst. You cannot reach it by yourself, for it exists in part as protection against pain and does not give up its secrets easily.

"Is it really me—my unconscious?" you ask unbelievingly.

"It is really—or unreally—you," he says.

You recall that the mind has been compared to an iceberg, the unconscious described as the part that lies beneath the surface. Most people go through life, you realize, never knowing the true depths of themselves. You compose a letter, which you will never send, to some of your friends who you wish could live more happily. It goes:

> Dear Sir [or Madam, as the case may be]:
> Meet your unconscious. Don't die in ignorance of nine-tenths of what you feel. If you deny this part of you, life is hell. If you accept it, life can be beautiful.

You sign the letter *Someone who loves you.*

"It's what I *don't* know that's been hurting me all these years, isn't it?" you ask. "What I know will never harm me."

"Agreed," he said. "You are here to make known what has been hurting you, what was once known but became unknown."

You are beginning to understand how this part may harm you if you ignore it too long or too defiantly.

You feel that the analyst would dismiss you forever if he found it out but, in an effort to understand your unconscious, you turn again to the textbooks. You, who are plunged into deepest misery, laugh wildly as you read that your mind is chiefly bent on seeking pleasure and avoiding pain. This is the famous pleasure principle described by Freud.

The books tell you that there stirs in you constantly, undiminished from childhood, the unceasing urge to fulfill some wish that will bring you pleasure, such as being held close to your mother, or selling your sister into white slavery so she will no longer be a rival, or sleeping with your father so you can show your mother you, too, can have babies. All of this you eventually find out to be true, although it takes you months to admit that such feelings exist in you, much less that they are pleasurable.

Your psyche is always trying to help you fulfill these wishes, which arise from your instinctual desires. The wishes focus on two goals: self-preservation and propagation. All else is sham.

Your desires prod you, as though to say, "Come on now, do something to ease my hunger." This stimulation causes you pain and you attempt to get rid of the stimulation and return as fast as possible to a natural state of serenity.

Thus the main purpose of your unconscious mind is to obtain prompt fulfillment of your need and no nonsense about it. When you were a child this was obvious. You were after pleasure at all cost, the devil take anyone's feelings.

Naturally (or perhaps unnaturally) as you grow up and must maintain what has passed these many warlike years for civilization, you learn that you cannot give in to your impulses. And those impulses are something to shake the stars! They include, among other acts, indulging in sexual intimacy with anyone in the immediate vicinity, be it father, mother, sister, or brother; stealing anything that catches your eye from anyone who passes by; and doing away with anyone you do not want around, for whatever reason.

Your trouble, you realize, is that you have not given up *all* of these primitive desires yet.

You dare to mention this to the analyst, saying, "It's quite a struggle, isn't it?"

"The battle begins the day you are born," he says. "You learn, frustration by frustration, that if you want to get along with others, you must think not of what pleases you but of what pleases your parents, even though it may bring you pain."

You find out, by further reading, that your mind like all Gaul is divided into three parts: the conscious, preconscious, and unconscious. There is also another trio in what Freud called "the psychological scaffolding." This is made up of your ego, superego, and id.

Your ego and superego are partly conscious, partly unconscious; but your id, where your instincts originate, is completely unconscious.

If properly directed and used by your ego, your id makes life wondrous, for from it springs your creativity, spontaneity, and originality. It can help you achieve a full, enjoyable life if you are able to handle it wisely.

But if your id is oppressed too fiercely by your superego, or, as it is popularly called, your conscience, you are in trouble. You may suffer much psychic and physical pain.

In this drama of the psyche you think of the id as the hero who needs someone to direct him; the ego as the heroine who tries to control the id; and the superego, when it gets out of hand, as the villain. Your superego is the voice of your parents as they tried to help you grow up, and later it becomes your very own. It is admirable when it speaks softly but can cause horror if it becomes a roar.

Each part of your mind serves an important purpose. Your id gives you strength and power. Your ego provides the ability to look at the world around you and use what you need. Your superego allows you to criticize and judge, to develop humor, to consider the rights of others, to put into artistic form the impulses arising from the id, be it via painting, writing, or designing an outer-space missile.

Now that you understand all this intellectually, you do not feel the least bit better. You wonder what has gone wrong in your life to produce such suffering. Why are you lying helpless on the couch, victim to strange, unknown enemies, alone and bereft in a heartless world?

"Why, why, why?" you wail to the analyst.

"Why what?" he asks.

"Why do I suffer so?"

"Technically, because of your repressions," he replies.

"What are they?" you ask.

Once again he is silent, so back you go to the books. You find out that "the direct cause of psychic suffering comes as a result of repression." Repression takes place when your conscious, usually at the behest of your cowardly conscience, says nay to an unconscious impulse and tosses it back to the unconscious.

You ask the analyst, "Does everybody have repressions?"

"Repression is natural and necessary," he says. "But when the unconscious becomes overburdened with too many repressions, you suffer emotionally."

"What makes for overburdening?" you ask.

"If you are forced to grow up too harshly or swiftly; if your parents fail to help you slowly to give up some of the desires the unconscious automatically assumes is its right to have fulfilled," he answers.

What Freud pointed out, you think, is all too true: "In bringing up children we aim only at being left in peace and having no difficulties, in short, at training up a model child, and we pay little attention to whether such a course of development is for the child's good as well."

It is not easy to grow up, you realize. Even with the best-possible parents, it is not easy to grow up. With a mother and father who cherish you and help you to master destructive wishes, it still is not easy to grow up. It is merely that much harder when your parents do not understand their own desires.

But grow up you must, you sadly conclude, unless you want to stage a one-man return to the jungle, giving up the half-step out of it the world has taken since the dawn of civilization.

"Please describe the unconscious to me," you ask the analyst, hoping what he says will agree with what you have read.

The silence is cold indeed.

You decide that the man who can first explain the unconscious clearly to another will deserve the Nobel Peace Prize. Perhaps it cannot be described to anyone—you can only know it in yourself.

But this much you have garnered from your reading: *the unconscious has no sense of time.* All the wishes and memories of your past, from the first moment of repression onward, whirl in it like sheets of paper in a wind-tossed world.

Yesterday is as today. The screams of the nightmare from which you awakened at dawn this morning hold your screams at the age of four months when you felt hungry; your sobs at the age of six when you weren't allowed to go to a party because you stole a piece of cake at home; your tears at sixteen when a favorite aunt died.

Only this moment counts to your unconscious. It is "Now" land, the land in which children dwell. The future does not exist for children. They refuse to accept, "Not now, later," because for them there is no "later."

You always thought of children as miniature monsters, to be avoided like the surgeon's knife; but now you look at them with new respect, for they give you countless clues to your own feelings. You listen to them as you visit married friends, become astounded at how children do not hide what they feel and how they accept violence as natural.

You visit the home of one couple who are worrying how to tell their six-year-old son that his uncle died of a heart attack.

The father, after much inner struggle, sits down with the boy on a sofa, says to him gently, "Uncle Jack has gone to heaven for a much-needed rest."

The mother interrupts: "Why not tell him the truth? He has to learn sometime and it should be from us."

Whereupon the father says solemnly, "Son, your Uncle Jack is dead."

Whereupon the son looks at his father and says just as solemnly, "Who shot him?"

To children the "drop-dead" routine is a natural one, especially when applied to family and friends. You visit a couple who have just brought a new baby, their third son, home from the hospital and proudly show him off.

The youngest boy, three years old, looks scornfully at the baby, issues the order, "Take him back to the hospital. We don't want him."

When his parents refuse to oblige, he sits glued to the television set, refusing to eat supper. Following a religious show, he turns to his mother, says, "Well, if you won't get rid of him, I hope he dies and goes to heaven."

His older brother, age six, is far better behaved. He

takes his mother aside and says confidentially, "I know how you have children, but how do you *not* have them?"

To his father, who has helped create the new star of the family show, he says, also in greatest confidence, "I hate you. Why don't you go away for good?"

You think how this little boy, should he be lying on the couch twenty years from now, will undoubtedly become highly indignant, even horror-struck, should the analyst dare to suggest that he in any way resented the birth of a younger brother or the presence of his father. He will profess only deep love for both, believing he has long forgotten how he felt the day the baby arrived, only really never having forgotten, for the feelings will remain, later to be hurled at others far removed from the original crime.

You see these feelings in children, but you cannot quite accept them in yourself. It is small solace to know that, along with every other adult, you suffer from "infantile amnesia": the forgetting of painful childhood memories. Just as you lose consciousness when physical pain becomes too intense, so when psychological pain becomes unbearable, you also lose consciousness—but in a different way.

Children also do not hide the fact that they, literally, want the moon. You are driving one evening with a couple and their two-year-old daughter who suddenly sees something new to her rising in the sky.

"What's that?" she asks in wonder.

"The moon," says her mother.

"I want it," she demands as though it were a toy.

Luckily at that moment it disappears behind a cloud. "The moon got lost, honey," says her mother.

"Oh," says the little girl.

Five minutes later the moon re-emerges in full brilliance. The child claps her hands joyfully and cries out to her mother, "You found it for me! Now give it to me!"

To the little girl her mother is far more powerful than the United States government or the winds that blow the clouds away from the moon. The little girl believes that her mother will grant her every wish, just as, long ago, you too thought that of your mother.

Now, years later as you lie in confusion on the couch, you face the unarguable truth of your unconscious, seeing how much like a child it is—lawless, selfish, impulsive. It recognizes no moral codes. It always seeks the path of least resistance.

There is another part of you that searches for a quiet look at what lies in the world outside. It wishes to fashion your unconscious desires in ways other men will admire, to help you become more thoughtful. This is the part that has brought you to the couch.

"Psychoanalysis is such a struggle," you groan once again to the analyst.

"But the noblest struggle of all," he says. "Just think: after millions of years, man has finally found a way to get acquainted with his unconscious."

It finally gets through to you that, as you make something conscious, you are then able to think about it. Obviously, you cannot think about unconscious wishes; the very word "unconscious" means "unthinkable"—in more ways than one, you conclude bitterly.

Thought will bring freedom from emotions that have kept you in agony. Thought will allow you to know the strength of what you feel, and use it to your advantage, not your downfall.

Thus you may become a conquerer of life, not its victim.

The Unlaid Ghosts

You plod in, propel yourself sullenly toward the couch, wonder where to start on this dismal, damp day.

"It's sure lousy out," you begin in brilliant fashion.

He is silent. You continue: "I don't know why, but I feel exceptionally forlorn today—as if no one cares whether I take another morsel into my mouth or fade away in famished despair."

He still says not a word. Here you are, pouring out your torn and anguished heart while he sits, unmoving as stone.

You say sarcastically, "Every analyst should have a sign posted at the foot of his couch which reads: *My heart bleeds for you. I understand how deeply you are suffering at this very moment. Now proceed with your thoughts."*

He says nothing and you know you must go on. You have learned the lesson that everything you tell him conveys something. Your remark about the weather, your opening pitch, so to speak, tells him that *you* feel lousy.

The words you unconsciously select to use, be they about poetry or poker, give him a clue as to what you are hiding that makes you feel as you do.

"I'm depressed," you announce.

"I couldn't have guessed it," he says.

Outraged, you sink into the gloomy sea of silence. Finally he throws you a word-preserver, saying, "Depression is unexpressed rage, turned on yourself. Say what comes to mind and perhaps the depression will disappear."

So you talk about how your job irritates you, how you cannot bear it one more day; you speak of your feelings toward some of the people with whom you work, and he helps you to understand that these are feelings you have carried with you from childhood, that the anger you feel does not belong to the present but is a hang-over from long ago.

You realize that there is no reason why you should feel strongly about unimportant things. Anything that evokes deep feeling must hold echoes of the past.

And only as you say what comes to mind, no matter how pointless it seems, letting one thought lead to another and another, can you reach for the memory behind the memory behind the memory ad childhood infinitum. That is where you are headed, willing or no.

This was Freud's first great discovery: that those who came to him for help, as they talked of whatever arose in their mind, uncovered feelings they had never dared to express, following which depression, physical pain, or nervous anxiety disappeared.

When the analyst first urged, "Say everything," you replied facetiously, "Perish the thought that a thought should be stray!"

But as you trace the delicate web formed by your associations, you find that there is no such thing as a random thought. There is always a reason—sometimes several—why you have brought up an idea or mentioned a specific number or used a certain word at this particular moment.

A sharp pattern lies under your patter, discernible at first only to the analyst's sensitive ear, but in time discernible to your own. You come to know that you speak on several levels at once. An apparently innocent remark referring to something that took place only yesterday may have bearing on what is taking place between the analyst and you and may also represent a feeling that existed in you as a child.

You are describing to the analyst a party you attended the night before at which a prominent American psychologist told a story that struck you as delightful. The psychologist visited Vienna at the time when Freud's theories, with their focus on sex, first shocked the world. He made an appointment to see the creator of psychoanalysis, was late in reaching Freud's home.

He explained apologetically, "I am tardy because the streetcar was delayed. It was so crowded that I was forced to sit next to a filthy old man and was afraid I'd get contaminated."

Whereupon Freud asked quietly, "And are you afraid you will get contaminated by *this* filthy old man?"

And when you have told the analyst this story, he asks, "And are you afraid you will get contaminated by the filthy old man who sits near you?"

"Certainly not," you protest as your cheeks burn.

But you begin to see that nothing is accidental or coincidental. You bring up what is meaningful to you unconsciously. From your associations you may know what you fear and at what you rage.

You leave one session feeling that the analyst is wrong, unreasonable, and perverted to dare to suggest that as a child you competed with your mother, wanting to steal the limelight from her. But you say not a word of reproof.

You start off the next session with, "After I left here yesterday, I got into a fight with my boss and told him off."

"Whom did you really feel like telling off?" asks the analyst.

You grin. "Consider yourself told off."

"Not at all," he says. "Tell me exactly what you wanted to say to me."

"Since you asked, I will. I was furious because you implied that I wanted to be the center of attention in the family, even to making my mother take a back seat."

"All children feel that way," he says. "I am asking you not to hide from yourself what is natural, for it is the deception that is making you unhappy."

You feel relieved. It is not just you who are selfish and demanding but all whose emotional needs are not fully met when they are children, which probably includes every member of the human race. That afternoon you apologize to your boss for your arbitrary attitude.

The analyst listens to every word you speak, both seriously and in jest, helps you understand just what you were up to all those unfortunate years when your distorted personality was being formed. He helps you decipher the new language of free association, a language based not on intellectual logic but on emotional logic, which, you discover, is governed solely by the law of your wishes.

You use the words you know, but you use them differently. You have been taught to use words to *conceal* what you think and feel. You must unlearn this, use them to *reveal* what you think and feel.

Sometimes you coin words that never existed or combine words or mispronounce them or give them new spellings or put words together in a nonsensical phrase. At first you are embarrassed by what you believe to be sheerest stupidity on your part. Then you come to treasure the slips as one of the ways your unconscious helps you understand more about yourself.

The dross of daily conversation—the pun, the crazy remark, the slip of the tongue—is the pure gold of life on the couch. There you accept the height of nonsense as the depth of truth.

On the days you feel weary, you are often most psychically productive, for then your thoughts flow quite freely. Fatigue seems to lower your resistance. The descriptive-feeling words rise more easily to your mind, and slips of the tongue follow closely upon each other like waves of an angry ocean.

You are talking about the escapades of Diana Barrymore as described in the best seller *Too Much, Too Soon.* You berate Miss Barrymore for her many amours.

"That Biana—" you begin contemptuously, then stop in amazement. "What do I mean—Biana? There is no such name. I meant to say Diana."

"What comes to mind?" the analyst asks.

"I don't know," you say, puzzled. "That's a crazy slip."

But there is no such thing in analysis as a crazy slip, for every slip signifies that the unconscious is trying to make itself heard. So you start to associate.

"Let me see," you say. "I substituted a 'B' for a 'D,' probably thinking, 'bitch.' I also think of 'Biana,' for some strange reason, as a pun. By-anna. Oh! I remember something."

"Yes?" says the analyst.

"Last night at a party," you continue, following through on your associations, "I met a friend whose name is Anna. She came with her husband. He got very drunk and started to flirt with me."

You add hastily, "Even though he is very attractive and I know their marriage is miserable, I rebuked him. I went 'by Anna.' Like a poker player says 'by me.' "

The analyst comments, "So when you reprove Diana Barrymore, you are really reproving yourself for perhaps a fleeting wish to be like her?"

"Hoisted by the petard of my own unconscious," you remark ruefully. "Sometimes I wish it weren't so strongly on my side."

"Whose side would you have it be on?" he chuckles.

The more slips you make, the faster you speed along and the more knowledge you gain of yourself. It is knowledge of a different sort than you learned in college but a knowledge far more important to your happiness than that which enables you to win $64,000 by answering questions about Civil War history.

Not only is it more psychologically profitable, but it is more fascinating to study your own unknown history. A new world of riches opens before your very senses, an imaginative, inspiring, free world where you can wander unfettered by the chains of conformity, civility, and servility.

But to reach it, you must realize that everything you think is important, even the passing thought you deem not worth your breath to spill out. Sometimes you say impatiently, "I don't know why this comes to mind because it's unimportant," and lapse into silence. The analyst knows at once that what you were about to say is extremely important.

He may ask what it is or wait until you bring it up at some future time, which you will. For in analysis, as Freud pointed out, "A thing which has not been understood inevitably reappears; like an unlaid ghost, it cannot rest until the mystery has been solved and the spell broken."

The longer you are in analysis, the more freely associations flow. Like chords in music, one association leads to and blends into another, stirring your memory so there is no order to the seasons or years but only the merging of powerful emotions.

The fragrance of a gardenia corsage given you the previous night touches off remembrances of the sweetness of your first kiss at the age of twelve, and that kiss is tied in memory to the tenderness of the first "I love you" at the age of sixteen, which takes you to a forgotten hurt: the breaking up a love affair when you were twenty.

Sometimes you halt when painful thoughts intrude. Nobody, whether stretched out on a couch or standing in a witness box—both places dedicated to truth—wants to admit feelings of jealousy, hurt, and rage. You fight to protect the image of yourself as a proud but gentle soul, no matter how high a psychological penalty you pay.

Your dreams lead you most directly to the unlaid ghosts. Each dream contains an important message from your unconscious which must be decoded, for it is written in symbols, the language of dreams.

The economy of a dream is fantastic. A dream can bring you pages of information about yourself in one brief image.

A ragged patch of red material becomes a dress worn by a woman whom you met the day before who reminds you of a friend who wore a red dress the day before she got married, a day on which she came to you sobbing, saying she was not sure she wanted to marry the man she had chosen, and asked your advice, and although you knew reasons why you did not like him, you said nothing, and now she has written you that she is getting a divorce and you are upset because you feel you should have warned her in the first place.

At first you insist your dreams are no part of you. When the analyst asks you to talk about a dream you say, "Why should I? It's only a dream," and flip it out of mind.

"But it comes out of you. You are the dreamer," he tells you.

"It's so simple, I understand it clearly," you insist.

"If it was so simple you wouldn't need to dream it," he says.

Reluctantly you describe a dream or two, just to keep him happy, although you still believe it just a pleasant fairy tale you spun at night for your own amusement. It does not mean a thing, and it is ludicrous for this stranger who sits behind you to imagine it holds any deep meaning; he is really stretching for it.

It takes time, quite a bit of it, before you accept dreams as very much a part of you, a part you might often prefer left in slumberland.

The stuff of which dreams are made merely starts with the action of the dream. As you tell of what each detail in the dream reminds you, out whirl your hidden wishes and fears.

Your dreams are dull to everyone but you and the analyst. People become bored when you tell a dream because the experiences are so very personal to the dreamer that they lose all meaning to others. Nobody else can feel the emotions in your dream evoked by a particular city, street, person, or deed.

You find that your dreams are sparked by something your unconscious has selected from the hundreds of things you did or thought or said the day before. It is a something you had not thought of as particularly important but which carried a deep tie to your past as portrayed dramatically in the dream.

You tell of one dream that makes even less sense to you than most. "I was walking down the street when an organ grinder came along with a monkey on his back. The monkey jumped to my neck and wouldn't let go until I had given him some money. Then I was walking down the same street, but now I held the organ grinder's wallet which was full of hundred-dollar bills. I thought, 'I must get this back to the old man.' "

You sum up cheerfully, "That's all there is to it"—famous last words of all who do not want to face their dreams, words that indicate you have not even started to understand the dream.

"Associate to the details," he says, also cheerfully.

"The dream means I have stolen money from some old man and feel guilty about it," you offer as interpretation, still, unconsciously, trying to stall.

"What about the words, 'organ grinder'?" he asks, putting you back on the track.

"He was an old man, tattered and torn. An old, old man." Tears suddenly come to your eyes. "I used to call my father 'old man' as an affectionate name. I adored him, even if he did slap me occasionally. I miss him terribly since he died."

You wipe away the tears. "He left me what I thought quite a lot of money which I didn't deserve."

"What about the monkey that climbs on your back?" asks the analyst.

"What about it?" you ask.

"I'm not a mind reader," he says.

"I'm not so good at reading my own," you grumble. "But I'll try. Let's see. 'Monkey on my back.' That's a phrase used about someone you feel is a burden. In the dream someone is on my back and I pay him to get off."

"Perhaps someone to whom yesterday you handed a large check for last month's analysis," he says. "Someone whose insistence that you face deeper feelings might well be a monkey on your back."

"Present company is always excepted," you wisecrack.

"Quite the contrary in psychoanalysis," he repeats, for the hundredth time or so. "Present company is very much the target of your feelings. By becoming aware of how you feel toward me, you find out your hidden feelings."

The dream showed that you resented paying the analyst for revelations undoubtedly unpleasant at times; showed, too, you felt you were robbing your father to pay the analyst, for you had been using some of the money he bequeathed you, and somehow you know with certainty, he would not have approved.

The dream held other feelings too. You bring up one of them, saying, "At times I am a monkey on the back of my mother. But how can I be both myself and the monkey on my back in the same dream?"

"In your dream you are, in part, every one in it," he says. "You are the dreamer. Each person, each animal, represents some facet of your feeling."

Dreams should satisfy both the actor and author in everyone, you think, for you fashion your own script, different each night, and play every part. You act out your most fantastic wishes, turn the tables on anyone you choose.

The quality of your life outside dreams is nothing like the one within them. You have thought of yourself as a peaceful soul who cannot bear to anger anyone. But each dream is bloodier than the last as you devise ways of murdering strangers who remind you, in queer distortion, of people whom you once vaguely knew, or who represent mangled and crippled versions of yourself.

Much of the symbolism in your dreams is sexual. Since your feelings about your body and the bodies of others are apt to be among the most repressed, it follows that these feelings will find outlet in dreams.

At first you deny that your dreams in any way reflect your sexual feelings. Then you realize that if you want to hold on to the illusion that you possess no hidden sexual yearnings and that the dreams you spin at night, full of serpents and big, gaping holes, belong to someone else, you may do so—but it is your own self you are misleading.

Every detail of a dream brings new revelations. Each number, each unit of time, refers to something so important to you that you must hide it in a dream. When a strange compulsion grips you, like washing your hands too often, or an object, such as a squat vase, stirs hatred, the feeling goes back to some forgotten but vital experience in your life that you relive in this symbolic way. Dreams will lead you to it. The compulsion disappears as you discover its dark roots.

As you track down the meaning of a dream it is like searching for clues in a mystery story that will lead you to the murderer. The murderer of course always turns out to be you, although in each dream this comes as a complete surprise. You are always the last one you suspect.

It is in your dreams that your deepest passions erupt and from your dreams that you trace life's overwhelming hungers. Reaching the heart of a dream is not simple because of its many distortions and disguises. You think you have fathomed a piece of truth but suddenly you know it is false, and then, often, just as you are about to give up, you grasp the essence of your feeling.

Nothing is too absurd or fanciful for a dream. It plays tricks on you, conceals meanings in puns, condenses an entire experience in one word or even half a word. It tries to trick you in all ways as your psychic sentinels, the ego and superego, in their unconscious capacity, still work to protect you from the pain of truth.

The analyst reminds you, as once again you are reluctant to set off on a dream, "Freud called dreams 'the royal road to the unconscious.' "

"It's a damned rocky one," you say.

"But rewarding," he replies.

Not by Words Alone

An icy day brings the first freeze of winter and you walk into the analyst's office shivering. Your nose is slightly stuffed and you apologize for sounding nasal.

"Sometimes I have difficulty breathing," you explain. "Usually when the weather is chilly or when I am threatened by a cold.

"Which is almost always," you add with a sniff.

You then wipe a smudge of dirt from your wrist, wondering how it got there.

"Did the dirt bother you?" the analyst asks.

You look worried. "I don't like to be dirty."

Then you say in an amused tone, "I hear my father's voice ordering me to be clean. He was a tyrant about personal cleanliness. He would fly into a fury if I dressed sloppily or my hair was not carefully combed. Once when I was about to go to school he grabbed a comb and pulled it through my tangled hair."

You are quiet, remembering the scene with mixed feelings, pleasure at his caring how you looked and pain at the pull on your hair. You say, in further remembrance, "When he felt particularly outraged at something I did, he would call me a little stinker."

At this moment your hand flies to your nose as though to protect it and you sniff loudly.

"What are you smelling?" asks the analyst.

"I'm *not* smelling," you say angrily.

"I realize that." He chuckles. "You are not smelling because you have stopped up your nose so you cannot smell. What are you *not* smelling?"

Suddenly you hear yourself saying defiantly, "I'm not a stinker. He was a stinker for calling me one," and you uncontrollably burst into sobs.

This is the first time you have given way to such wild emotion in front of the analyst and you are ashamed, but stronger than shame is the spurt of fiery anger against your adored father that throbs through your veins.

"I—I'm sorry," you say, reaching for your handkerchief.

"What for?" he says in a low voice. "If you feel like crying, cry."

This permission to cry makes you feel even more shaken. No one has ever told you to go ahead and cry if you felt like it.

As the sobs subside, you explain: "Ever since I can remember he called me a stinker when he was displeased with something I did, whether it was keeping him waiting five minutes or not dressing fancy enough for a party."

"He probably first called you that when he was trying to help your mother toilet-train you," the analyst says. "It's a descriptive word for that period of your life. And then, with all the might at your small command, you probably tried to stop being 'a little stinker,' at the same time furious at him for insisting you control the pleasures of your body."

A new thought excites you. "And one way to fight back, maybe the best way I knew at the time, was to shut out the offending odors by stopping up my nose."

"Then, if he called you a stinker, he was a liar because *you* could not smell anything," says the analyst.

He adds, "You resented being toilet-trained, as every child does, because it was the first time you were made to control bodily impulses that were pleasurable. You would have been angry, but far less so, even if your parents had been kind and patient—but you would have been more able to handle your feelings. If a parent is irritable the child becomes confused and rebellious when toilet-trained."

"And may fight with his body as well as his mind?"

"Why not? His body is for him to use in his behalf too."

"What a stupendous relationship between body and mind!" you marvel.

"It happens all the time in a thousand different ways. We can never separate body and mind in action—only intellectually," he says. "The unconscious, besides being the storehouse of repressed wishes, takes care of your body's functions such as breathing, the beating of your heart, the operation of your digestive system."

"I can understand that if I had to be conscious of every breath, every heartbeat, every turn that food took in my stomach, I'd have little time to look at Sid Caesar," you say.

You never really thought before just how closely body and mind worked to help you maintain self-esteem in the face of the follies of yourself and others.

You ask, "If something upsets me, does my unconscious try to help me feel better through my body?"

"It attempts, through any part of your body that may be directly or indirectly involved, to make up for the distress, to defend you against further assault," he explains.

He adds, "When you catch cold, that is one way of preventing yourself from doing something unpleasant. When you complain of something you must do in the future which you do not want to do, you always come down with a cold, I notice."

All this from a sniff. You understand why Freud advised analysts against taking notes while those on the couch poured out their terrified hearts. Not only did he believe the analyst could not get as close to you if you felt he was scratching away with pen on paper but if the analyst concentrated on writing he might miss many of the gestures of your body that betray the inner soul.

Freud knew you give away your secrets with far more than your voice. It was one of the reasons he believed so deeply in psychoanalysis. He wrote, "He that has eyes to see and ears to hear may convince himself that no mortal can keep a secret. If his lips are silent, he chatters with his finger-tips; betrayal oozes out of him at every pore. And thus the task of making conscious the most hidden recesses of the mind is one which it is quite possible to accomplish."

Thus it is not only by words you tell about yourself but by sobs and sniffs and sneezes, and by chest-beatings and wheezes, and by sighs and the closing of eyes.

Your actions, which sometimes speak far louder than the words, convey intangible feelings that elude words but are nonetheless real, just as in the first years of your life you talked with your eyes, the tone of your voice, and the movements of your body, without speaking a word.

This is why psychoanalysis can never be adequately described. Not only does much of it hold no meaning except to the two persons involved, but much of it you cannot put into words, even to yourself.

You can only feel it.

Little Orphan You

You are still gripped by the terror of a nightmare as you walk into his office.

"I woke up screaming this morning," you say in disbelief, as though screams play no part in your life, awake or asleep.

You shudder as you recall the dream. "The door to my room slowly opened and, one by one, enormous cockroaches crawled in. They headed for the bed, swarmed up it and over my face and chest. I screamed myself awake." Your hands fly to your eyes to hide the horror of the scene.

"Associate," is his laconic reply.

"Yes, sir," you reply. By now you have the hang of free association. Instead of thinking up logical explanations and interpretations, you relax and freewheel your way from thought to thought.

"Cockroaches are the ugliest bugs alive," you begin. "They move in, one by one, devouring me, blotting out my life."

Suddenly you become even more horrified by what you now think than at the dream. You exclaim, "I don't believe it!"

He waits for you to inform him what catastrophe you have recalled with such revulsion.

You relieve his suspense. "Last night I was visiting some friends and their cute baby crawled across the floor gurgling in delight. I leaned over and said affectionately, 'Why, you little bug, you!' "

"What is it you don't believe?" he asks.

"According to my blasted associations, I feel that little babies are bugs who will devour me," say you, who have younger brothers and sisters.

"Yes, just listen to your words about the cockroaches. 'They moved in, one by one, devouring me, blotting out my life.' That's quite an apt description of how a child feels when he sees his successors at his mother's breast. At this point in his life this is the most terrifying thing he can experience, something that seems to him complete abandonment."

You have read in the books that insects often symbolize brothers and sisters, but this is the first time you have the feeling that a bug is not just a bug. You say slowly, "A bug then, may be a smaller child, someone you want to squash tight in warm embrace, fearful lest you squeeze the life out of it, and at that moment you hear your mother's voice complaining, 'Stop hugging the baby so tight. Do you want to hurt him?' "

You protest to the analyst, "But I hate bugs while I adored my little brothers and sisters."

"Haven't you said you thought your mother preferred them to you?"

"She did," you declare emphatically. "I felt like Cinderella. I might as well have been an orphan."

"You felt like an outcast," he says.

"Exactly," you agree, grateful that he understands your loneliness. Then, in a rush of feeling you confess, "I never felt anyone cared whether I lived or died before I came here. You make me believe I am not less than dirt."

At this point you choke up. You cannot tell him of other, deeper feelings about him that consume you, of the moments without end you long for him. If you did not think he would catch you at it, you would haunt his doorstep. Just feeling that he is near, even though he is not aware of you, reassures you.

"Thank you for being on my side," you tell him, soft ardor in your voice.

"Analysis is a unique situation," he says. "There is no other relationship like it."

"I certainly couldn't talk like this to anyone else," you say. "They wouldn't understand. I can tell you the craziest things, but you never think I'm crazy. In fact, quite the opposite, for it is my crazy thoughts and dreams out of which you help me make sense."

This, above all, has welded you to him. You can even spout gibberish and he will listen intently. It is the damndest paradox of all that, sometimes when you think you are making the most sense, he accuses you of wasting time, and when you believe you are the craziest, he thinks it most valuable.

It puzzles you that he does not act in any way like your parents; and because he does not, you say things you could never say before, even to yourself.

"I'm learning to trust someone," you tell him.

Then you cannot help adding, "More or less."

He trusts you and asks you to learn to trust yourself. You tell of an automobile accident in which you were involved coming home from a visit to friends. The car was so damaged it had to be towed away, but luckily no one was hurt.

"I knew I should have taken the train back," you say. "All the way out the driver had been describing accidents to which he had been a party, none of them his fault, of course. My sixth sense told me we would soon be in another and, sure enough, we were. Why couldn't I have trusted that sixth sense?"

"Sixth sense?" he says. "What's the matter with your perfectly good five senses? You heard him tell you he was accident-prone."

"I guess I was feeling guilty at heaven knows what and wanted to be hit," you say bitterly.

The analyst has been talking more to you in recent sessions, but even when he is silent you no longer think of his silence as criticism, negation, a way of cutting you down to infant size. You realize he had to know something of your unconscious before he could begin to help you put together the psychic pieces, and thus his role as earnest listener.

You feel you have finally found someone who cares what you do, and in turn you care about him as you have never cared for anyone.

You cannot hide your awareness that you more than care for him. Your dreams will not let you. You dream of embracing him, holding him close. You tell him this and he accepts it without censure or surprise and points out it is the way you felt about your parents as a child.

You are embarrassed by this wave of feeling for him. You bury it until Christmas, at which time you give him an expensive gift, which he accepts under protest only after you refuse to take it back.

"You shouldn't give me a present," he says. "I feel the way doctors do in some African tribes. When the patient gets better, the doctor gives him a present."

This makes you love him the more, convinced he is the most compassionate soul alive.

He can do no wrong. If he plotted to rob a bank you would beg him to let you help. When your family or friends attack psychoanalysis, it is as though they attack him personally, and you turn on them with a vengeance that should alone belong to the Lord.

You would like him all for yourself. If you knew, gracefully, how to murder all his other patients without arousing anyone's suspicion, you would do away with them at once. You understand, of course, that he has to accept other patients in order to earn a living, that if he had the choice he would spend all his time with you. So you forgive him.

You hate all members of his family, and you hate his secretary too. You realize that they preceded you into his life so he is stuck with them. It would hurt his reputation to get a divorce or abandon his children, and he does need a secretary so the ring of the phone will not interrupt his session with you.

When for some utterly nonsensical reason he has to call off your appointment, perhaps to attend a psychoanalytic convention in a distant city or visit his dying mother, you are as devastated as though both your parents had suddenly perished within five minutes of each other.

You wander around, lonely, forsaken. You stay home from work, tell your boss that you are stricken with some strange malady—which is no falsehood. You find yourself at the zoo, standing in front of the caged, miserable monkeys and the haunted, apathetic bears, all longing for homes from which they have been heartlessly torn.

That night you get deliriously drunk for the first time in years, revel in your rebellion even though you later pay for it as you lie on your bed moaning in physical and mental misery.

When next you see him, blazing rage flashing from your bloodshot eyes, you accuse him of deserting you, and why would he not, for how could he possibly want a spineless, abject, complaining creature who can only spew out self-pity, the meanwhile twisting and turning on the couch like a mewling infant in the crib? Even though he is of the "suffer-fools-gladly" profession, there are some limits to his endurance. Aren't there?

But before long you again feel confidence in him and this lasts until summer. When vacation is mentioned, you sink into a stupor. You separate for the summer—which you are certain will be your last on earth—with mock bravado.

You smile sweetly and say to him, "I hope you have a wonderful time." Under the barbaric lie you think, "How can he bear to plan enjoying himself while I am left behind in such despair?"

You spend the summer telling yourself you do not care if he did desert you. You do not even care whether he comes back at all. Then, the next moment, you are afraid he will never return, that his plane will crash or he will be killed in an automobile accident.

You visualize the plane as it bursts into flames in mid-air and plummets to the desert below, the automobile as it flies off a cliff and sails into the bottomless sea.

Then you are horror-struck at your treachery. For you

have become aware that every fear hides a wish that has been repressed. This first hit home when you were telling him that sometimes you peered underneath the bed at night to make sure no one was hiding there.

"Or perhaps in the hope that someone is there?" he asked.

"Why would I want to find a man there?" you said nervously.

"Is it a man you expect to find?"

"I never heard of a woman hiding under a bed, did you?" you said in sarcasm.

He ignored the question. "With whom did you sleep the first years of your life?"

"First with my father and mother, then my brother."

"You might wish your father and brother, the first masculine objects of your love, were still with you," he said.

"I certainly miss them." Tears came to your eyes. "My father is dead and my brother lives hundreds of miles away."

Shortly after, you saw again how the wish was bound to the fear when a friend of yours, married to a man who occasionally disappeared on all-night binges, phoned to beg you to come over.

"Dick has been gone for hours and I know something dreadful has happened," she said in ominous tone. "He's probably been in a terrible accident and is lying on the side of the road bleeding to death."

Alarmed because this was the first time she showed such fear, you raced to her home believing that some sixth sense on her part foretold that peril pursued her husband. You sat up with her until two o'clock in the morning, at which time her husband staggered in, unshaven and extremely plastered, made his way to the bed, and soon was snoring loudly.

She looked at you in embarrassment and said not a word, and you understood that, for the first time, her anger had broken out in the form of fear. She had unconsciously wished her husband injured to pay him back for hurting her.

And your fear that the analyst will perish, masks the wish that he die because he has deserted you. Now you become consumed by unholy guilt because you have wished him dead. How can you possibly feel so ungrateful after all he has done?

You can and do. The unconscious is not a sometime thing.

You spend precious moments plotting revenge. You will quit analysis, never again lie on his uncomfortable old couch or face his insipid paintings. It will be proper disgrace for him to lose a patient in mid-air (better than *your* losing *him* in mid-air).

You do not quit, of course, because you would not dream of depriving yourself of the pleasure of snarling at him when he returns.

Snarl you do. He expects it. He knows that the temporary separation has meant a kind of death in your unconscious, and is prepared for the fullest measure of your wrath.

And for this, too, you love him, with a love that is new. There is a love you feel for a man, another for a baby, and still another for your parents, brothers, and sisters; but this is a love apart from the rest.

You love him because he does not reproach you for anything you say or think or do; because he sanctions all your feelings, understanding that you are what you are and you do what you must do.

You love him because he gives you the feeling, for the first time in your tempestuous life, that you have worth and dignity. He never upbraids you for anger or tears, even though you have put the Furies to shame and have wept enough to irrigate the Sahara.

You love him because he honors every word you speak; to him nothing you say is unimportant or meaningless.

You love him because he makes you feel that the people in your life are as real to him as they are to you. He remembers far more than you do of what you tell him over the months, and is much more sympathetic toward your mother and father than you ever were. It is through his eyes that you start to see that they have endured as much pain as you, each in his own way.

Even though you are paying him, there is a quality in him all the money in the world could not buy, the feeling that, above all else, he desires to ease suffering.

"You show such concern for me," you tell him.

"Not 'concern,' " he says. "That would be a burden to you."

You realize how you chafed for years under the yoke of your parents' concern. No, it is not concern.

Is it love that you feel for him? Whatever its name, if it has one, the feeling makes it possible for you, eventually, to love someone else, to love in an enduring, intimate fashion.

What difference, then, what you call it?

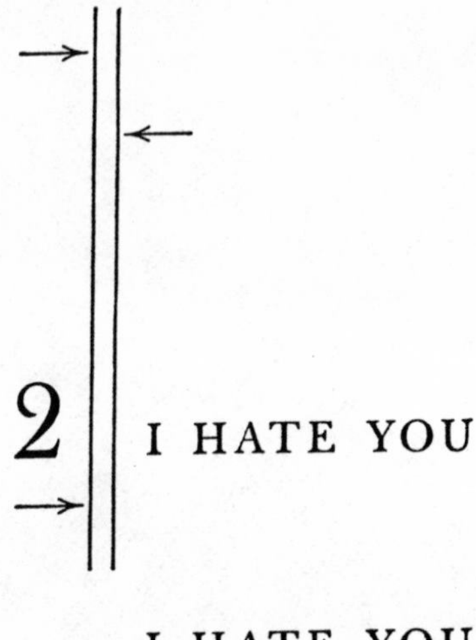

2 I HATE YOU

I HATE YOU

I HATE YOU

What Is This Thing Called Love?

You rush into the analyst's office, breathless. You can hardly wait until you reach the couch, so eager are you to tell him the sensational news.

You try to be calm as you describe what happened. "Over the week end at a dinner party I was introduced to a tall, aesthetic young man who is an artist, and it was love at first sight for both of us."

You add shyly, "He even proposed. I think we have a good chance of making each other happy."

There have been several such romances in your life, but something always interfered to prevent each one from becoming the love story of the century. This, however, is different. You feel the ecstasy of first love for this stranger who is Prince Charming, Sir Galahad, and Frank Sinatra all in one.

"I never had this feeling before," you say dazedly to the analyst.

"Pardon me if I remind you of several times in the past when you reached these heights, only to plunge quickly downward," he remarks unfeelingly.

"That was some other patient," you say hastily.

"I think not." He dares to argue.

"You don't believe this is love?" you ask angrily.

"Do you think so?"

"Please try to understand," you plead. "I'm sick of being by myself night after night, of one toothbrush on the rack, one coffee cup on the breakfast table."

"But you cannot use someone else as an escape from your loneliness," he says. "Loneliness is something to be solved within."

He is saying that if you sleep alone, night after night, in the midst of eight million people, not one of whom belongs to you, the greater tragedy is that you do not belong to yourself.

"I can't stand the torture of nighttime with no one next to me," you complain. "There can't be anything worse."

"One thing is worse," he says. "To have somebody next to you whom you hate. You must *know* the person whose body is beside you."

"Many people get married without knowing each other very well," you object.

"And when they do know each other, they discover too late they do not want to spend the rest of their lives sleeping together," he says.

You think that maybe courtship *is* sensible, in that it allows two people to edge closer to each other in many ways.

"Some of my friends compromise by pushing away the loneliness of night with a temporary lover," you say.

"Yet this is not the answer if they want a lasting, intimate closeness with one person," he says. "It's often the way of avoiding love."

"Agreed," you sigh. "And that is why I am here, alone on a barren couch, refusing to compromise."

Then you ask, "What do you mean by 'love'? It seems to exist everywhere except in my life, in the movies and plays I see, in the books and magazines I read, in the music I hear. What is it?"

He says slowly, "Love means all things to all men."

You think of the old French proverb: "In love, it is like the old inns of Spain—one finds here only what one brings in." Each one brings to love the feelings fashioned of his dreams and desires. There are as many definitions of love as there are people.

You realize love is a highly civilized word, that man existed for millions of years, able to find a mate and propagate long before he could speak one word, let alone the tender word, "love."

"Do analysts believe in love?" you ask naïvely.

"We most certainly do or we would not be analysts," he says. "But we think 'love' a word loosely used. Sometimes what people call love is the stuff of childhood longings. It has little to do with mature love except to interfere with it."

"Aren't love and hate supposed to be close together?"

"When the two are so close you can hardly tell them apart, I doubt if the result can be called anything remotely resembling love."

"What is love then?"

"Let me ask you. How did you feel about your mother when you were a child?"

"I loved her, of course. As I do now. I would give anything to see her smile or have her bend down and kiss me on the cheek as she did when she was happy."

"Let's call that the blue of the rainbow. Did you have other feelings about her?"

"At times I got furious, when I thought she liked the other children better or when she wouldn't buy me the dress I wanted or when she made me come home from a party and all the others were allowed to stay late."

"The red of the rainbow."

You think a moment, then say, "Sometimes she seemed far away, in a world of her own, and I despaired of reaching her."

"The orange. And still other shades of feeling?"

"I was jealous of her when she came between my father and me."

"The green, of course. Aren't you forgetting another?"

"That's all I remember," you say.

"What about your rage at your father for coming between her and you, of your wanting only her in your world?"

"I don't think I felt that," you say.

"If you didn't, you're not human," he says. "The feeling is there, buried under layers of denial."

"Perhaps." You shrug your shoulders. It does not seem too important to you, although you believe he considers it a worse crime than matricide for you to deny a feeling.

He goes on, "If you add up all your feelings about your mother, you find quite a few in what you thought was the one emotion of love. Rarely is a feeling pure and simple. It is rather like a twisted rainbow of sensations, confused and diffused. You are here trying to understand your feelings in their contradictions and conflicts."

"Are you saying that I will understand what love is as I understand that I also hate?" You are puzzled.

"I am saying that what you have thought of as love is the love of the movies in which everything is solved with the first passionate kiss. In reality that's when problems begin."

"So I've wasted my time wishing I were like Marilyn Monroe," you say, only half joking.

"If you went around acting like her in public, they'd clap you in a home for the mentally retarded," he says.

"This is the most shattering of blows," you tell him. "You would have me believe that what I thought was true love in my teens, blossoming as we danced to the Casa Loma Orchestra and later, as we kissed under the stars vowing to be true forever, is a myth."

"Isn't it? What happened to this great love of yours?"

"He married some home-town girl and never moved an inch from where he was born," you say disgustedly.

"Why didn't you marry him?"

"He had no ambition."

"Do you think that's the reason?"

"I don't know," you say, truthful with yourself for a change.

"Your unconscious may have had something to do with it," he says.

"Damn my unconscious," you curse. "It has doomed all my romances to dust."

"Only so far," he comments.

"Will you please tell me why?" you plead.

"You'll find out for yourself in time."

"I know nothing at this moment except that you apparently don't approve of my trying to find someone to love," you say sullenly. "Do you expect me to have no sexual feelings at all? What am I supposed to do with my deep longing?"

"Why the urgency?" he asks.

"I'll burst with desire," you wail.

"If you do, you will make history," he says. Then he sighs. "Sex and money. They serve so well to hide other things."

"What do you mean?"

"The urgency of your desire is due to many things beside your natural need."

"Like what?" you demand.

"May I say once again: that is what you are here to find out. There is no simple answer."

You say dubiously, "I'm afraid if I examine my feelings too carefully, I will lose the exciting, passionate quality that is part of love."

"You won't lose the quality," he says, "only the urgency."

He adds with a chuckle, "You remind me of a joke. A psychologist, testing a man, asks what a white handkerchief reminds him of. 'Sex,' the man replies. The psychologist asks in surprise, 'Why does a white handkerchief remind you of sex?' The man answers, 'Everything reminds me of sex.' "

The joke didn't seem very funny at that time.

And This Thing Called Sex?

"I won't say what I'm thinking at this moment," you tell him, your voice carefully controlled.

"Please do," he urges. "We'll get along faster that way."

"Something has upset me," you begin, then are silent.

So is he, so on you go. "I was almost here when I suddenly had to go to the ladies' room and I went into a dingy restaurant a few blocks away. Scribbled on the walls of the toilet in flagrant obscenity I found that fascinating but forbidden four-letter word."

"What word?" he asks.

"Please!" You are alarmed. "You don't want me to say it, do you?"

"Why are you so frightened of it? It's a word in common use—possibly the word uttered more often with stronger feeling than any other."

"Common is right," you mutter.

"Why do you have trouble saying it?"

"Because I feel ashamed."

"Shame is a convenient way to hide deeper feelings."

"The word is obscene," you protest.

"Calling something obscene is another way of dismissing your real feelings."

"Is anything *not* a way of hiding my feelings?" you demand.

"Talking about them," says he.

"It's not easy to use words you have been taught are dirty," you offer as excuse. If one excuse does not serve, you are only too eager to dredge up another, proud of the quality and quantity you can muster.

"That, too, is an—" he starts.

"I know," you interrupt: "an excuse. But I find it impossible to use such words."

"I'm not asking you to go around defiantly using four-letter words," he says. "I'm only asking you to examine your feelings about them."

"They're so—so disgusting," you say.

"Why should the natural functions of the body be treated with disgust?" he asks.

"I don't know. I've always felt that way, though," you say.

"I'll bet you haven't," he says. "A baby has no such feelings."

"Children *don't* think their excretions disgusting, do they?" you say in sudden realization.

You recall visiting friends whose two-and-a-half-year-old daughter insisted on being bathed by you. She gurgled in glee as you soaped her, slapped water over her tiny body, then sat her in your lap to dry her off with a mammoth towel. She looked up at you and said in mischievous delight, "I'm going to twinkle on you."

Knowing this was the word her family used for urinating, you were at first shocked. Then you remembered that Freud had said this desire showed that a child liked you; it was his way of bestowing on you a precious gift which, as yet, he had not learned to view with disgust.

So you took the little girl's wish as a compliment, patted her small behind, and got her off your lap as quickly as possible.

She then refused to go to bed, excited by your visit. "One more ride on my horsie," she said, mounting a miniature toy horse that rocked her back and forth.

"Get down," ordered her mother. "You've had enough. I'm dizzy from watching you ride that horse."

"One more," said the little girl.

"Tomorrow," said the mother.

"Now," said the little girl.

The mother got up from her chair, walked over to the child, and explained, "It's one hour past your bedtime. I said 'tomorrow.' "

"Now," insisted the little girl and you could but admire her persistence, thinking how greatly children need this quality in order to combat the giants surrounding them who often seem (and perhaps are) selfish and brutal.

Slap! The mother's hand cracked against the cheek of the little girl who burst into heartbreaking sobs. You wanted to pick her up, gather her to your breast, and comfort her, but you dared not oppose the mother.

One more ride would have enabled the child to work off the excess excitement she felt at the presence of a stranger. Instead, she was punished for trying to find a way to rid herself of tension. Yet, you understood, too, the irritation of the mother who had no doubt given in to the child many times that day and deserved a few quiet moments in the evening.

"Children know no shame until taught it," the analyst tells you. You try to see yourself as a child, possessed by feelings now fathoms deep beneath the façade of compliance.

At first you are just this side of shocked at how casually the analyst accepts the four-letter words you have been taught not to utter. But it is because of this that you get the courage to express some of your feelings.

You learn not to be ashamed of anything you feel. Instead, you become ashamed when you hide what you feel.

You realize that it is not just human nature to want to do the forbidden but the forbidden that *is* human nature.

"I always believed my childhood a time of great innocence," you say.

"Not on your unconscious life!" he wisecracks. "It was a time of great un-innocence. Your desires freely expressed themselves without your conscience to block them."

"You mean that, as an adult, I prefer to think of children as innocent because I wanted to forget the frightening feelings of my childhood?" you ask in wonder.

The innocence of children is a myth maintained by adults to keep them from awareness of the childish feelings that still haunt them, you conclude.

You nurtured the illusion that you suddenly developed feelings for the opposite sex when you were ten and a precocious sixth-grade Don Juan kissed you passionately at a Saint Valentine's party. But in analysis you discover you had bodily stirrings years before, probably ever since you were born, if not prenatally, but felt these feelings evil because the objects of your desire were members of your family.

"All the sexual feelings of my life form my libido, don't they?" you ask, wondering if he will curse you for using what he believes the dirty word, a technical term.

"Must you?" he groans on cue.

"I must," you say. "Why, this has become such an important word that there is even a street named in its honor —Libido Lane, somewhere in California."

"It's certainly the state most suitable to herald the concept," he says. "California, the home of the industry built on appeal to the libido."

As you talk of your feelings for your family, you find that many sexual or libidinous stirrings, aroused at a time you do not remember, still warm your blood.

They occurred when you had no way of releasing desire, for you were not advanced enough physically to imitate what you suspected your parents did. You could only dream, and rebel at the slowness of your growth, praying it would increase beanstalk speed.

As you grew up, you became aware of intense physical desire for the parent of the opposite sex, with a two-way undercurrent of seduction in steady progress. Just to complicate matters, your brothers and sisters got into the act so that everybody was seducing everybody else, at the same time denying the seduction by temper tantrums or more subtle displays of anger such as contempt.

"We repressed the desires, is that it?" you ask.

"You were a sure bet to do so, not being a member of an uninhibited family in the back woods or the slums of a city," he says. "But all the while your primitive, savage self could not help screaming at your conservative, prudish conscience for depriving your body of pleasure; for your unconscious, first, last, and always, protects the body's pleasure."

"Thank heavens something does," you mutter.

When the suggestion that you might possibly have had a slight yearning for your father is first brought up by you-know-who, your prompt, unequivocal, emphatic, unalterable answer is, "Never!"

"Incestuous feelings have been with us since man blinked on his first dawn," says the analyst. "Even today some primitive tribes give in to them, indirectly."

"I know," you say, not willing to let him think you a complete ignoramus, even though you will not come right out and admit you wanted to sleep with your father. "Like the women in Polynesia, according to Melville–Herman Melville, that is," you explain, in case he is not as hep to American literature as he is to the Oedipus complex. "In his book *Typee,* he says each woman of a certain tribe was allowed to live with two men. One, her husband, was an elderly man; the other was a young boy. She slept with both of them, no questions asked."

"This fulfilled her unconscious wish to possess both father and brother–the woman's fantasy world come true," he says.

"You can hardly expect civilization, which gives women only job opportunity and equal pay, to match that!" you say sarcastically.

As you begin to face your feelings, you think, "Well, perhaps there is a little of Hamlet in me."

Months later you tell yourself, "But of course. What did I think that feeling was?"

Who else was around for you to love? It would not occur to you to fall for your best friend's repulsive father, who was mustached and smelled of an odious shaving lotion. Your own was far more tempting, besides being always near at hand, even though he could sometimes be infuriating.

Also, memories persisted of tender care given you in earlier years before he decided to devote so much time to screaming at you and slapping you for talking back. You have a faint impression of his holding you close, rubbing his golden beard against your cheeks, kissing your face hungrily.

Such love does not go unrequited. Especially when you have strong desires of your own that need expression.

You must, at length, admit, although this is among the severest of blows, that your intense intellectual curiosity at bottom is sexual curiosity. Your concern with high-sounding theories and pursuit of the philosophical are merely devious ways to cover your interest in a subject far more intriguing.

You are not among the first to arrive at this conclusion. The words "to know" in the Bible often have a strictly sexual meaning.

Your great curiosity concerned what happened between your mother and father at night. You slept in their bedroom until you were two years old so, although you have no memory of it, you must have seen or half seen, heard or half heard, ghostly figures in the dark, and what they were doing undoubtedly struck you as the greatest mystery of all time.

"A child doesn't understand what's happening at night between his parents, does he?" you ask the analyst worriedly.

"Probably not, but he will certainly use his imagination to try to figure out as best he can just what is going on," he says.

"Is it harmful for a child to sleep in the same room as his parents?" you ask.

He replies, "I don't believe it's as harmful as it is for the child who does not know what is really going on, who has to dream up his own distortions. Somehow I think the truth can be assimilated."

He adds, "I think the greatest harm comes when you deny that anything intimate occurs between parents. In countries like India, children are forced to sleep in the same room as their parents because of poverty. But at least there the children do not pretend that nothing takes place."

You laugh embarrassedly. "In a way I have always pretended that my parents had a platonic relationship. That is, if I thought of it at all."

Many of your feelings are not easy to admit, for they focus on everything you have been taught is taboo. But in analysis they are considered natural, not evil.

And so it is that you discover that "sex," the word that packs more punch than any other, encompasses far, far more than you dreamed.

The Fact of Fantasy

"All this talk about *reality,*" you say contemptuously. "What is real to me is only what I have experienced. Otherwise, it does not exist."

He is silent.

You try to tempt him. "Of course there are certain things no one can deny as real. That we have to eat to keep alive. How babies are born. And that there is a physical difference between men and women which serves the purpose of perpetuating the species."

He bites at the bait, which means he must be feeling expansive, for he replies, "There are even some who will deny as real all the things you mention. For example, not quite everybody accepts that the difference between the sexes is for propagation. So-called homosexuals act like children who, at a certain time in their lives, do not know the purpose of the difference. Homosexuals cannot accept reality because of their fantasies."

You scowl, ask, "What do you mean by 'fantasy'?"

"Analysts speak of fantasy as of, by, and for the unconscious," he says. "It is not the conscious, Walter Mitty kind of fantasy of which you are aware. That's a daydream. The deeper, unconscious fantasies can only become conscious through analysis; those are the kind we're after here."

"How many fantasies do I have?" you ask.

He laughs. "As many as you need."

"I probably have a million of 'em," you say. "Sometimes I feel all is fantasy."

"Not quite," he says, "or you'd be in a mental hospital."

When you first start analysis, you see no clear-cut line between fantasy and reality. It is all one world, albeit a world you do not particularly cherish.

Slowly you begin to realize you are living in two worlds. One is the world in which you eat, sleep, and work. The other is the world of your hidden feelings.

"I feel like three people," you say. "One is the person society knows. The second is the person I know. The third is the person I don't know but am getting to know. They're not separate either, but each one is permeated by the others and it's all very confusing."

Your world of fantasy becomes, during analysis, more real than the real world as you see how, over the years, you were driven by the secret desires that gave rise to the fantasies.

Everyone has fantasies, using them at times to escape reality, which can do with a bit of escaping. Your fantasies have been part of you ever since you first opened your eyes and tried to make sense out of a world that awed you, puzzled you, troubled you, pained you, angered you, and sometimes seemed just plain crazy.

Your fantasies increased as you became engulfed by an ocean of "Thou Shalt Nots" that extended from exploring your own body to making mudpies with a little boy your mother thought undesirable, probably with good reason—although there is not any reason with "no" in it that seems good to a child. Deluged with "don'ts" and the feeling that you were wicked if you disobeyed, and realizing the world was no longer your pearl-filled oyster, you tried to figure out why this tragedy overtook you and just what you could do about it.

One of your oddest fantasies, as it comes out on the couch, is that thoughts are all-powerful. A child believes he has but to wish something and it is done with a wave of his tiny, imperious hand. Ghenghis Khan was a Milquetoast compared to the average child.

You have held on to this fantasy to some extent and are often afraid, still, to think a thing lest it become fact. You finally realize that, up to this point in our uncertain history, thought rays still lack the lethal power to strike anyone dead.

In your world of fantasy your deepest emotions find expression; there you live, if not properly, at least fully.

The world of fantasy is completely megalomaniacal. Everybody exists for the sole purpose of being your willing slave.

You are the center of the universe, the one and only, the Almighty, the shining sun, the deep blue sea, and the glittering stars. Everything about you is haloed and all the things that belong to you are treasured, including your excretions, which are your most precious possessions, for they are your very first creations, excelled by nothing you have fashioned since.

You are the hero of heroes, but you are also the victim

of all victims, spiked, bloody, bowed, beaten, and brutalized by villains wicked beyond belief.

It is most natural, if you feel injured, to seek revenge; therefore you devote a large part of your time to wondrous ways of avenging yourself on those who have attacked you, and you become without a qualm the most vicious of killers. Next to you, Jack the Ripper is Pollyanna. You plot murder as though ordering from a menu; the command "Off with his head!" is as mundane as "Bring me a hamburger."

You think it is only the innocent stranger you wish to obliterate; but as the analyst prods you into more and more free association, you find that beneath the disguise of innocent bystander lurks your mother or father or brother or sister or cousin or uncle or aunt or whoever else interfered with your pleasure as a child.

You start with your father, for he is the first offender of your life, the first to come between your mother and you. Every baby wants his mother to himself on a desert island, the whole world shut out. So you kill off your father in fantasy, bury him deep, banish him to the furthest planet.

You deny that anything even remotely resembling sexual intimacy took place between your mother and father, except perhaps the one time you were conceived. You do not go quite as far in this fantasy as some who, as they wander around mental hospitals, insisting they are Jesus Christ, manage to do away with even this one time, for, born of a virgin mother, they rid themselves completely of the need for a father.

In fantasy you have all the babies you wish by your father. Also, with the greatest of ease you snatch your brothers and sisters from your mother, announcing, "They are *my* babies."

There is no doubt but that your mother is the most dreadful woman ever to live, even throwing in Medea, who killed her own children; and you would make your father a far, far better wife. Therefore, although you regret it, though you need her desperately, your mother must go too.

When all's thought and said in fantasy, your mother must die because she has committed the greatest of sins—borne other children; this is betrayal beyond comprehension. She should have been content with you, whether you were first or last or somewhere in the middle of six.

Above all, in fantasy, you wish to be a good mother to all the outcasts of the world, the abandoned children who suffer as you suffer. You want to be a much more compassionate mother than your mother was to you. You will show her and the entire world what a marvelous mother you can be, so they will have to acknowledge you as the greatest mother of all time and erect a monument to you bigger than Abraham Lincoln's in Washington, D.C.

There is no limit to your selfish wishes, no boundary to your vicious desires, no horizons to your hungry needs. They stretch in endless procession to infinity and you are determined to fulfill them all.

This is the fantasy world you face in analysis. This is the world of unreality that you must slowly give up if you want to live in harmony with yourself and other men.

In the beginning you kept using the word "really," saying over and over, "This is how I really feel," or, "This is what I really mean." Now you think differently about what is real.

The moments in your life when you believed yourself *really* happy, the short-lived, ecstatic, out-of-this-world, sensational moments, were those in which you were *unreally* happy. They held the spell of wild, child happiness, not the glow of contentment free of violence and anger.

"I feel like Humpty Dumpty," you tell the analyst. "My fall off the wall is the fall from fantasy to reality. My illusory self has been smashed into a million pieces."

You add, "Sometimes I feel that I can never be put together again. But I seem to be putting myself together, with a different me emerging."

Then you ask, "Is *this* fact or fantasy?"

He says, as you knew he would, "Do you have to ask?"

Repeat Performance

You are lying on the couch saying shamefacedly, "You were so right. That man with whom I was so desperately in love has turned out to be impossible."

"When it's desperate, it isn't love," says the analyst.

"How could I have been so mistaken?" You are ashamed of yourself. "I just couldn't take it any more."

"*What* couldn't you take?" he asks.

"While I was growing up, I lived under a constant barrage of questions fired by my parents—what are you doing, where have you been, where are you going, when will you be home, whom are you seeing? I couldn't wait until I was old enough to flee this daily inquisition.

"So what happens? This man, who at first seemed sweet and concerned about my welfare, suddenly starts questioning me all the time. He turned into a carbon copy of my parents."

You add, with horror, "I would have been living

through the same kind of pathological prying from him, had I married him."

"I thought you liked him because he reminded you of your father," says the heartless analyst.

"In looks, not deeds," you retort. "He had the same golden hair and merry blue eyes. How could I know he would turn out to be like my father in behavior too?"

"Your unconscious knew from the start," he says. "It takes in at a glance all that is familiar, that it wishes to have once more."

"It's so much wiser than I," you mutter.

"It *is* you," he says, "if you'll only meet it."

"I'm meeting it halfway these days," you protest. Then ask in despair, "How in God's name can love turn to hate so quickly?"

"God's name has nothing to do with it. Your name has," he says. "At first you saw only what you wanted to see—golden hair and blue eyes."

"Why didn't I see the other quality before I got so deeply involved?"

"Perhaps you did and that was one reason you got involved," he says.

"What do you mean?" you ask.

"When you first met him, you recognized something familiar—or familial. A 'concern for your welfare,' you put it. As you got to know him, this became 'pathological prying,' against which you rebelled as you had rebelled against your family. You were not in love. You were acting out."

"Acting out? What's that?" You are mystified. This is a term new to you, although you thought you had read of everything likely to come up on the couch.

"What you've just described," he says. "Getting into situations that gratify your fantasies."

"Why would I want to do that?" you ask.

"For a host of reasons. It brings you temporary release from anxiety. It springs from something that has angered you, so it is a form of rebellion. It is also a way of deceiving yourself about dangerous feelings, a way of hiding pain."

" 'Oh, what a tangled web we weave, when first we practice to deceive'—ourselves," you groan.

You discover that much in your life has been an unconscious seeking of the familiar, followed by strong protest against its hateful parts. This explains why you get into situations that at first seem exciting, then feel trapped. You *are* trapped—by the phantoms of the past.

You think of a friend who married a man believing that he was as charming as mortal could be and that their life together would put heaven in the shade.

The honeymoon was brief. The husband came home one night drunk, cracked his wife across the face, and ordered, "Get the hell out of here." She fled to a hotel, fearful of being further hurt, but returned the next morning not knowing where else to go. When he came home from work, he apologized, asked her to try again. For several days they lived in armed truce until he once more got drunk, beat her, and threw her out. In spite of his continued brutality she remained with him a year before she finally left.

You tell this to the analyst and ask, "Was this acting out?"

"Of course it was," he says. "Your friend was getting vicarious satisfaction from her husband's violence. He was acting out her fantasies too or she would not have endured it as long as she did. I would wager their life together in many ways was similar to the one in which she grew up."

ve got a crystal ball that works backward," you say, amazed, for you recall her parents fighting angrily for years before her mother finally walked out.

"No crystal ball," says he. "Just an understanding of how the unconscious works."

"What was she acting out?" you ask.

"I couldn't possibly know her fantasies. They belong to her alone. She was probably playing, in part, the role of her father, in part the role of her mother, in part her own role. She was also assigning roles to her husband. Perhaps he stood for the part of her that might have wished to scream at her parents but never dared."

"One of the most extreme forms of acting out is murder, isn't it?" you say thoughtfully. "Killing someone must be the acting out of many fantasies."

"The deed of murder holds in it many, many moments of supreme terror and even more supreme repression," he says, "repression that must explode in violence."

You discover that many deeds, which people commit and you think obscene, are the acting out of fantasies of childhood. They are obscene because they remind you of feelings which you were taught were shameful.

When you hear of a young girl marrying a man old enough to be her father you think, "How absurd can you get?" forgetting your dreams as a little girl of marrying your father. The Peeping Tom you think so disgusting is trying to see what all children wish to see. Knowing what causes these acts does not, of course, make them more acceptable; but it does put them in perspective, and puts you in fuller control of your hidden wishes.

As you face your desires you can understand that it is these same desires, more intensified, more urgent, that drive people to extreme acting out. If someone has had a childhood where few of his emotional needs are met, fantasies may explode like firecrackers.

The words "acting out" are well chosen because what you do is a devastating caricature of yourself and the people in your life.

"I'm appalled at how I unconsciously imitated in exaggerated style different characteristics of my mother and father," you tell the analyst.

"That's how a child learns—by copying those around him," he explains, "adding to this, of course, his own inimitable impulses, including the wish to be different from all others."

"Does everyone act out?"

"As you grow up, if you are not too emotionally deprived, you learn to use your own good sense, to criticize, judge, and select for yourself," he says. "But if you are angry, if important emotional needs have been neglected, you do not think or judge too clearly. You continue the caricatures."

When you repeat the same deed over and over, only to have it end in dismal failure, be it a romance or the work you do, you are acting out. You are driven by forces you do not understand and cannot control.

You are giving one repeat performance after another in grotesque imitation of an original experience or experiences which you have buried deep. You know intellectually that you should stop but are unable to restrain yourself from repeating the act, useless in one sense, useful in another. It is useful in that it allows you, in a distorted drama which only an analyst can understand, to tell what disturbs you. It is useless in that it does not ease your torment, indeed often deepens it.

During analysis you try to stop the acting out that has

dominated your life. That is the only way you can understand the fantasies that lurk behind it.

You cannot become aware of fantasies while you hide them in the acting out. You simply do not possess the psychic energy to both act out and also face the fantasies, for each takes a heavy psychological toll.

Also, while you act out, you cannot see what you do, for an actor cannot observe himself. He may be able to express many feelings as he plays his role, but he cannot see himself. Acting out, in analysis, is, plainly and simply, a resistance to seeing your real self.

When one of the roles you play becomes particularly powerful, it may actually take over your conscious life, as with the famous "split personalities." There is nothing mysterious about a split personality. Those who become two, or even three or four, personalities are acting out facets of persons important to them in childhood.

You chose to caricature certain aspects of your mother, certain aspects of your father, and a few choice ones thrown in that you garnered from a grandmother or two and a few aunts who made a fuss over you when you were small.

It is as though you have been possessed. You recall one of the oldest theories about insanity—the disturbed soul was "possessed" by demons who invaded and took over his person. This was not too bad a hunch, you think.

The demons were the parents whom the possessed person caricatured, from whose spell he could not break free. He could only act out his fantasies about them in a form everyone else thought crazy but which made sense to him.

"My acting out arose out of desperation," you tell the analyst as though that would excuse it.

"It usually does," he says. "It follows some deep hurt that is repressed."

As you become aware of what has hurt you, the acting out stops, ending the destruction which is all it ever brings in its wake.

What was being destroyed? Part of your real self.

While you are busy caricaturing others, you as a person disappear.

Less of a Patient

"Stop crucifying me," you groan.

He has just pointed out how strongly you competed with your mother for your father's love or with your father for your mother's love. It does not matter which, for you are guilty of it all.

"If my eyes do not deceive me, you are not nailed to that couch," he says.

Suddenly, after all the love you have felt for him, you are stunned to realize that you hate him at times.

True to his instructions to tell everything you feel, you inform him, "At this moment I hate you. I don't understand how I can love and hate you at the same time, but I do."

"That is what's called ambivalence," he says. When *he* uses a technical word it's acceptable.

"Then I've felt ambivalent about many things in life, but most of all about you," you say sweetly.

He has started to pour salt into your psychic wounds. Recently, you feel, he has been pinning you down as if you were a butterfly, examining your every quiver as you struggle in vain to free yourself from the sharpness of his stiletto insights.

At first he approved of everything about you, even unto your desire to write bad poetry, but now you can do no right. Once you could complain that he was hurting your sensitive soul, or berate him for not giving you the comfort a fortuneteller would; and though then you feared he might heave you out, sometimes now you wish he would. But if you dare even hint that you suffer after one of his malicious interpretations, he merely treats you as he would a child who is throwing temper tantrums over some imagined slight.

In the beginning when he was silent you were afraid he had dozed off. Now you pray he would fall sound asleep instead of listening so carefully, then probing into your psychological wounds after the words you have uttered lead him to the sites of scars.

Not a slip of the tongue or a graceless gesture escapes his eagle eye. You have a habit at times of covering your eyes when you speak, and he calls attention to this as well as to how you keep your legs carefully crossed, or clench your fists, or twirl your thumbs. Defenses all, he treats them as covering you-know-not-what traumas although you would bet the price of analysis they are hideous.

He either keeps silent when you wish he would speak, or he interrupts when you would like him to shut up. As he points out—needlessly, of course—the fallacy of one of your fantasies, you cry, "Say, whose analysis is this anyhow? Let *me* talk."

He hates you, you feel, or he could not possibly treat you as he does.

You accuse him. "You hate me, don't you?"

"Who hates whom?" he asks.

Do I hate him, you wonder? Is this what is known in the higher (looking upward from the couch) circles as "projection," the psychological turnabout in which you accuse others of feeling toward you the way you feel toward them?

You thought you bore him a love that nothing could destroy. Could it be that as you moved (rather, as he pushed you) deeper into the intricate pathways of your psyche, your love congealed just a bit?

It is difficult, you confess (to yourself alone), if not downright impossible, to feel totally tender toward someone who, no matter how courteous and gentle his manner, is intent only on exposing the ugly, suffering parts of you. He seems to be taking away everything, giving you nothing in return but the cold shoulder, and even that you cannot see since he is out of sight all the time.

Reluctantly you admit your warm feelings of adoration are now slightly chilled by occasional blasts of cold hatred. This is what you have heard parlor Freudians refer to as "the negative transference," as opposed to "the positive," during which you unreservedly adore the analyst. Negative, hell, you think. You do not feel negative, you feel downright murderous.

You stagger into his office, stare at this chameleon character. Once you thought his expression kindly; now he wears the leer of a porpoise whose mouth is wide-slitted in a perpetual smile—but a false smile. And his eyes, once soft and tender, have turned into the steely eyes of the shark, so unfeeling that they looked painted on his face.

"He is a brutal monster," you think, "and I despise him as the foulest creature on earth."

A minute later he asks if the light is too strong and would you like the curtains drawn and you think, "He is the most sympathetic, understanding person in the world, and how blind I am to have felt otherwise."

You love the analyst—hate the analyst, love him—hate him, love—hate. You seesaw in the turbulent sea of ambivalence. One moment you want to kill him with the paper knife left temptingly out on his desk, the next, to cover him with caresses.

He is crueler than Hitler, kinder than Christ. He is wiser than Confucius, more stupid than Lot's wife.

You admire him for his brilliance, yet there are moments when you are convinced that he cannot see what lies in ten-foot headlines under his nose. He is so intuitively honest you wonder how anyone can get that close to truth, but there are also times he is the damndest of liars.

Yes, perhaps you are ambivalent about him, and about analysis too. You want to face the truth—you do not want to face truth, you have to—you do not have to, you can—you cannot, you must—you must not.

But one reason you are lying on the couch, in ambivalence or other tortured mood, is the wish for greater peace and this you know will forever be illusion unless you accept the fact that you have feelings that are opposed.

"Hate and love exist side by side in your unconscious in apparent comfort," he tells you.

"In my conscious they fight like hell," you mutter.

This thing called ambivalence, the inconsistency in your soul, is an agonizing feeling to face. Before analysis you honestly (dishonestly) believe feelings must be black or white, that you either hate or love, that you cannot feel two or more emotions at once.

How wrong can you get? As a child you felt love and hate at the same time. You had mixed feelings toward your parents as they frustrated some of your wishes. You feel the same mixture toward the analyst as he, too, starts to frustrate wishes that must be denied if you are to know yourself.

One of the least lovable things he does is to ignore your psychic SOS's. Many are the times you beg him to make a decision for you, trapped in situations out of which you see no escape.

"What shall I do?" you plead.

He refuses to tell you, gives you not one clue as to which course to take, leaves you stranded in the quicksand of uncertainty.

You have heard the charge that psychoanalysis is dangerous because you fall under the spell of the analyst and follow his every suggestion. This is but a wistful wish on the part of the critics, for nothing could be further from truth.

In the first place, your herculean resistance keeps you from falling under anybody's spell except your own carefully woven childhood one. In the second place, the analyst will not give his opinion unless your decision is a drastic one that could cause you much pain.

You are furious when he will not advise you. You threaten, "If you don't tell me what choice to make in this crisis, I will hurl myself from the highest skyscraper, or take to astrology."

"Stop putting me in the place of a parent who decides for you," he says.

You understand that it would be perpetuating the old

familiar, fatal pattern in which you obediently did what Papa and Mama believed proper, all the while furiously resenting the domination; but you still wish that he would guide you.

Then you realize that if he did, part of you would lose respect for him, the part that wants to shed the skin of servility, the part you halfheartedly admit should be strengthened, not weakened.

"I'm impaled on the horns of a psychic dilemma," you announce. "I am begging you for advice, feeling I must have it; but at the same time I would resent it if you gave it to me."

"It won't help you if I tell you what to do," he says.

You know he is right, that when somebody else decides for you, nothing is really decided. You have come to him to help you stand up psychically, a feat which seems incomparably harder than learning to stand up physically.

Along with your desire to be told what to do, goes another wish: to be told what *not* to do.

Something in you begs to be restrained when you are about to take a step you feel harmful. You do not ask him directly to halt you; you plead in devious ways, such as by falling ill or sinking into a depression, thus paralyzing yourself.

But in spite of his neglect, in spite of his apparent cruelty, in spite of your occasional feelings of hate, you continue to give him the greatest gift you can bestow on anyone—your trust.

This slowly built pivot of psychoanalysis on which all else depends is constructed on a foundation of mixed feelings. That trust can survive, even though there may be hatred as well as love, for the analyst finally gives you the courage to look even deeper within.

Trust allows you to face the depth of your dependence on him. It is such a depth that you feel you have sold your soul into bondage. But the sale took place a long time ago, years before you wandered into his office.

You give up the psychoanalytic bondage as you give up the older bondage. This takes time because you are such a willing slave. It takes work, both on the analyst's part and yours.

You recall the feeling of a man treated by Freud who wrote that in his analysis he felt "less like a patient than a co-worker."

At first you wish to be a patient, insist on being a patient. You do not want to give up the illusory strength that comes from being comforted by someone else. But slowly you let go the demand to be a patient as you realize it does not help you become free.

Too, the analyst acts as though he expects you to be strong. Your parents considered you a freak who had to be alternately punished like a villain and humored like the village idiot. But here a man, for whom you have the utmost respect, treats you as an equal, considers your judgment as good as anyone's.

He considers your judgment so superb that most of the time he expects you to answer your own profound questions. You say angrily, when silence again greets a query, "I should know better by now than to expect an answer from you."

"When it's a question that only you can answer," he agrees.

Only you know the answers to the questions in your life, you grudgingly admit. Gradually you give up awaiting his approval for everything you say or do and begin to acquire the art of approving of yourself.

And although in the beginning it was as if he talked Greek and you Latin, slowly, slowly, you begin to speak the same language.

Do You Remember Mama!

You bring in a dream from which you have awakened with sheer delight.

By this time you know that dreams never, never, not even hardly ever but absolutely never, mean what they seem on first acquaintance. If you wake from a dream you think gay, you are due for a miserable jolt, for underneath the intoxicating illusion of joy always lies some repulsive repression.

You tell him with a certain amount of cheer, knowing you will lose it before long, "I dreamed I was riding up and down an escalator in a department store. In the middle of the up and down banks stood a long table piled high with delicious foods and I leaned over and heaped my plate high."

You sigh as you think of the endless pastries to which you helped yourself.

"Why the sigh?" he asks.

"My mouth still waters for those chocolate éclairs," you say. Then you add proudly, "Freud would call this a ferocious oral need, wouldn't he?"

"What's the matter with Mother Goose?" he asks.

"What do you mean?" You think, "There he goes again on Mother Goose," and you must reread it at once to discover what he finds so fascinating.

He is quoting one of the rhymes: "Goosey, goosey gander, where do you wander? Upstairs and downstairs and in my lady's chamber."

"So now I'm a goose," you say indignantly.

"I didn't mean that," he says, "although sometimes you're rather like an ostrich in the way you hide your head from the obvious."

"The obvious to you is not always the obvious to me," you reply with as much dignity as you can muster in the face of Mother Goose.

"Look at your dreams," he pleads. "Are you still denying that they are part of you?"

"Not quite so vehemently," you concede.

Over and over your dreams feature feelings of yearning for your mother, of hating anyone who comes between her and you. The analyst is asking you to accept that, at the heart of all psychic matter sits your mother, that your all-consuming hunger is for her, that unconsciously you would like to return to the first comfort and warmth you knew. It is the most stupendous struggle of your conscious life to face this as the simple truth, and yet you must if you want to give up the complicated deceits.

The hardest truth of all to take is the oldest one in your life—the longing to return to your first pillow of flesh. You have never had it so good since, and do you resent it!

You have spent your life running off in ten thousand

different directions to keep from running in the one direction you unconsciously wanted—to your mother.

Some of your hidden feelings hold a strong emotional quality, others you are able to understand at first only intellectually. It is comparatively easy to feel yearning for your father. It is not quite so easy to feel it for your mother, so deeply is this repressed, even though it appears in ways you cannot long deny.

You can see the desire clearly in others—always proof it exists in you—in those who greedily suck away at a bottle (socially acceptable because it now holds liquor) or frantically inject themselves with a constant flow of medicine or hungrily devour endless pills or more food than they need.

"A child may feel hunger for his mother in any one of his orifices—mouth, nose, anus," says the analyst. "For instance, the act of sodomy fills the hunger in one orifice."

"So homosexuality is hunger for the mother," you say in amazement.

Early in the analysis you had expressed contempt for a young man who was feminine in walk and gesture, saying, "He makes me uncomfortable."

"You mean you can't stand a man's involvement with his mother," the analyst had remarked.

At that point you did not know what he meant; you had room only for bitterness. But now, as you understand your own feelings, you become more sympathetic. You tell the analyst, "I'm not so furious any more at men who cannot love women. I realize that it isn't as simple as it seems."

"It isn't simple at all," he says. "Homosexuals, as Freud pointed out in his classic study of Leonardo da Vinci, carry from childhood a deep erotic attachment for their mother and are unable to love any other woman. They want to be like the mother they adore, whom they unconsciously imitate. They also live in terror of losing the mighty instrument they possess, which they fear will be taken from them because they desire their mother so desperately."

"Can homosexuals be cured by analysis?" you ask.

"They have been," he says.

"It occurs to me that what I have always believed perversions are childish yearnings, all," you say.

"Plus anger at the mother who, it is felt, is constantly seducing but never carrying through on the seduction."

"No wonder the act of sex, as indulged in by unhappy people, never leads to happiness, because sexual fulfillment is not what they really desire," you say in wonder.

"As a matter of sad fact, Freud held that the incapacity to meet a real erotic demand is one of the most essential features of neurosis," he says.

"I will pardon you for quoting Scripture," you say nastily. Then you ask, rhetorically, "How could people who, emotionally, are still children meet an erotic demand, the privilege of maturity?"

"Unhappy people use sex as a way of trying to appease earlier desires," he muses. "If sexual intercourse solved problems, we'd all be happy as kings."

"It's the cabbages that get in the way," you say brightly. Then you add, for his benefit, "O. Henry. 'Cabbages and Kings.' "

"I know," he says with a sigh. "I occasionally read something besides Mother Goose."

Your hunger for your mother, when frustrated, made you fly into a fury. You thought you were angry at her because she favored the other children, but now you realize that the anger stemmed from your selfish demands.

"I thought I was angry because she deserted me," you say in a sad voice.

"I don't recall your telling me of any desertion." He sounds puzzled.

"Not literally," you say impatiently, wondering why he is sometimes so stupid. "She didn't leave me to the wolves, if that's what you mean. But when I was growing up she left me psychologically. That's worse than physical desertion."

"Come now," he says. "Your mother was always there. She gave you more than enough food. She loaned you money when you needed it. She couldn't baby you all your life."

"By the way, I was weaned at six months, she once told me," you say reflectively.

Then something occurs to you. "I have always believed no person could endure me, or I them, longer than six months." You add, "Quite a coincidence," knowing it is no coincidence at all.

"No wonder at the end of six months' relationship with someone, there has to be some kind of explosion," he says.

"Are you telling me I'm still in a rage?" you ask in a rage.

"No, you're telling me," he says. "Every baby is angry when weaned. This is his first rejection, and if it is not done tenderly he will scream in wrath all his life, one way or another."

"What about babies who are not breast-fed?" you ask.

"The bottle represents the breast, and when it is taken away, depriving them of the sensation of sucking, they are apt to become angry."

So, much of the deep anger you feel about things in your present life is "anger hang-over" from the days of diapers, belonging to the time when your mother left you crying in crib or cradle because she had to go to the store or visit friends or relatives or make love with your father. You were not able to understand that she might have a good reason to leave; nor could you forgive her for leaving. You only knew you were abandoned and felt a helpless fury.

This was a time you did not know the concept of love or hate, when you could put nothing into words. You only knew you felt a need to be comforted, and if it was fulfilled you were contented—if it went unfulfilled you screamed in rage.

The feeling of being abandoned has haunted you through the years. Often, when it becomes intense, you act with abandon, as though you would abandon yourself too. You try to draw attention to yourself through careless, violent deeds—not attention for the sake of attention, but to be once again drawn back into your mother's arms or at the very least drawn back from danger by her touch, even if an angry touch, for an angry touch is better than no touch at all.

By realizing how devastated you feel when separated unexpectedly from the analyst, to whom you have transferred feelings originally bestowed on your mother, you come to know this is life's greatest tragedy—to be apart from your mother when you needed her. You understand why so many murders occur when one person threatens to leave or actually leaves another. There is no greater torment than to be deserted.

Not long after what you felt to be the first big desertion, your brother was born and then you felt the betrayal complete. By that time, although you could speak, you would never have dared put into words what you felt.

Instead, you cooed over the new baby, decided you would adopt him as your own. As long as your mother would not be a mother to you any more, you would be a mother to your little brother, in accordance with a basic law in the land of the betrayed—if you can't have 'em, be 'em.

"I don't believe it," you say when the analyst first gives you these interpretations. "She couldn't have meant that much to me."

"Every mother means this much to a child," he says.

"Even if she was a Hottentot or a murderess?" you ask in disbelief.

"*Who's* the 'tot'?" He laughs.

"And I suppose at the age of six months I was also a murderess," you say sarcastically.

"You probably felt slightly cannibalistic," he says.

"Or criminally insane," you retort. "At least that's the way I would feel today if I confessed that my feelings were those of a baby screaming for its mother."

He is silent. You sigh in resignation. "It seems so much easier to admit feelings for my father."

"He came later," he says. "He was second best."

"You're always on my mother's side," you say defiantly. "Why is that?"

"I am on neither your mother's side nor on your father's side," he says. "I am not here as judge—only to help you understand what happened in your life."

Dump or Be Dumped

One morning you hand the analyst a check as payment for the past month. Then you lower yourself majestically to the couch, prepared to make an important announcement.

You proudly inform him, "I don't have one red or otherwise-colored cent left in the bank."

Half in jest, half in sadness, you add, "This may be the last check you get from me."

"You don't have to pay me right away if you need the money," he says, proffering the check.

"Oh, no!" You recoil as though from the touch of a tarantula.

You wish to be broke. That is what you find out during the session.

As soon as you finish the fifty minutes you rush out to make arrangements to earn extra money for further analysis.

But you are on a very special kind of kick, so a few

days later you decide what you have been doing professionally for years is no longer fit work for you. You must cease this dissipation of time and talent. As long as you cannot be what you wish—which is a Hollywood producer or prolific playwright—you will become a beachcomber, because it is ridiculous to throw away your life on mundane, monotonous tasks a robot could perform.

You tell the analyst, "I've decided to give up my job and be a beachcomber."

"It's a novel idea," he says. "But just remember how you feel after only a week end with nothing to do."

You have to admit that leisure hurls you into immediate shock. Week ends are unendurable; you have thought of forming a Week Ends Anonymous to get through them. Perhaps beachcombing is not your destiny after all.

Now you decide that what you need is to get married, that there is nothing like the love of a good man. You have made an agreement not to marry until the analysis ends, but there is nothing to prevent you from beginning to look for someone with whom to share the rest of your life.

You stumble on a man who is so unfit for marriage that even you cannot ignore it, and you inform the analyst that you are thinking of getting married. But so dismal is your effort that you cannot keep up the pretense for long.

Perhaps you could rob a bank, you think, and be hustled off to jail, where you would not have to worry about a dull job or getting married or how to pay an analyst. But you could no more rob a bank than climb the Himalayas, for you are constitutionally unfitted for both.

One morning you breeze into his office and announce gaily, "I feel wonderful. I have never felt better in my life."

"What is *this* about?" he asks.

"I'm as healthy as I will ever get, physically and psychologically," you say exuberantly.

"Oh," he says.

You elaborate further. "Those deep depressions that used to take me by the psyche and hurl me into the depths now never occur. I haven't had a cold in months."

Two days later your flight-into-health fantasy is shattered as you succumb to a steady, sickening procession of physical illnesses ranging from mild pneumonia to severe toothache. You also plunge into the deepest depression this side of suicide, making all others seem like rehearsals.

Now you *know* the analyst can no longer help you, for you have not been this psychologically or physically low since you first saw him. He has done nobly up to now, but the law of diminishing returns is bound to set in, even in analysis, you tell yourself.

You are not even sure any more that he *is* the best analyst in the world. You met a former patient of his at a party and was *he* a mess. You forget, in judging that patient, that no two people on earth can be compared, for not even identical twins have the same emotional life.

You have had it. You will no longer pretend-quit, as you occasionally have in the past. This is serious-quit. You have been the model of a model patient long enough and are ready to launch your own life. You are able to analyze yourself by now; you can reach the heart of any conflict that might conceivably arise, you tell yourself.

All these devious devices to end the analysis mean only one thing—you are striking deeply into hidden feelings.

You are trying to do what you have always done when life gets rough. You retreat into fantasies that in the past have served you not wisely but too well.

You use all your power to avoid facing what you feel. Luckily the analyst realizes that your innocuous attempts to break off are a way of asking him to hold you close, not to let you go. He knows that you are resorting to little dramas to tell him something, perhaps of your anger at being exposed to feelings too close for comfort.

He says merely, "What did you dream last night?"

You are only too eager to tell him. "I dreamed I was eating dinner with a man who got up and left me to dance with another woman. I threw my new squirrel coat over my shoulders in fury and walked out on him."

"You walked out on *him,"* says the analyst.

"I sure did," you say with great relish.

"And at this point you want to dump me," he says.

"Well—er—" you gulp, "well—er—"

"In the dream it was because I danced with another woman. Could it have anything to do with the new patient that comes after you?"

"Oh, is there a new patient?" you ask, wide-eyed.

"Unless you're struck blind on leaving this room, you've seen her," he says.

You have seen her all right, and she is so breath-takingly beautiful that sometimes you hide in the powder room so you will not have to face her. You had decided you would ignore the whole matter—that is, until this moment when you know you no longer can.

You find yourself saying belligerently, *"You* want to dump *me."*

"I do?" He sounds surprised. "Why?"

"You should be sick of me by now."

"Who's sick of whom?" he asks.

You recall how often the knowledge that fear masks a wish has been brought home to you. Is it your wish to end the analysis out of fear that he will call it an analytic day because of a lovely new patient whom he undoubtedly prefers to you? Your associations lead you to an ancient but nonetheless active feeling that your mother preferred the beautiful new baby who followed you.

He asks, "Is it that you want to be the one to do the dumping?"

"I *wasn't* the one to do the first dumping," you say indignantly.

"Did you make up your mind it wasn't going to happen a second time, that you'd show her you could get along without her?"

"I'd be damned sure no one else ever got the chance to dump me," you say ungraciously.

"I am not going to dump you," he says.

"That's what *you* say," you retort.

"What do you say?" He chuckles.

"I have nothing to say." You sink into a silence out of which you vow you will never emerge.

No one is going to dump *you*. You are the one who makes the getaway, calls the parting shot. Ever since that first desertion, imagined or not.

You decide to come out of the silence because you have thought of a remark too succinct to be kept to yourself. You say bitterly, "Dump or be dumped—the story of my life."

You add ironically, "Isn't that a lovely way to achieve happiness?"

He does not have to tell you, for, despite this current outbreak of childish feelings, you know that when you end analysis, it will be in a quiet, thoughtful manner. You will be fully aware of what you are doing, have talked at length about all your feelings.

The pitiful struggles during which you have tried to break away from analysis represent the same kind of flight in which you have always indulged when you feared abandonment.

They signify the sound of fury still raging within.

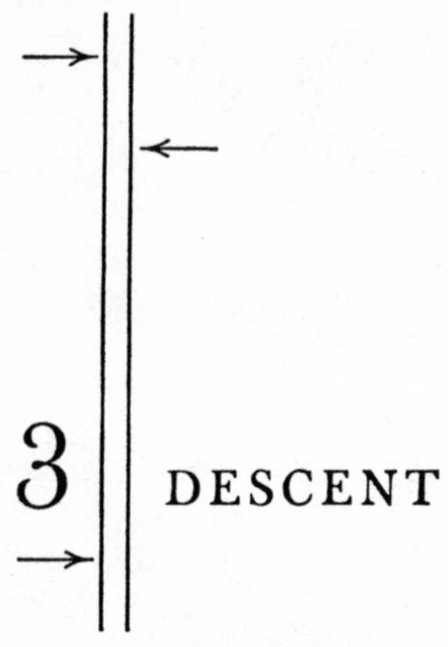

3 DESCENT FROM CLOUD NINE

The Importance of Being Stuffed

You walk into the analytic chamber one morning with head bent, throat sore, nose running. You have used the most plebian way available to mankind of laying yourself low, the common cold.

"I have a raging sore throat," you announce, flinging yourself on the couch and waiting for pity.

It does not come, of course. There is only silence. You swear the next time *he* catches a cold—and he is not above (or below) occasionally hauling one in—you will not be sympathetic as in the past but will ignore his sneezes.

Better yet, you will quote the Duchess' advice to Alice: "Beat him when he sneezes," and he will know exactly what you mean.

"I realize I said *raging* sore throat," you announce emphatically to let him know that you are well aware of what you have said, even though he pretends not to be.

"I *was* in a rage last night," you continue, determined

to give of yourself in spite of the fact that a pneumococcic death is, clearly, your inescapable fate. "A friend of mine called and begged me to have dinner with her and two other people of whom she is particularly fond. She said I could go home right after eating."

You swallow to ease your throat. Red-hot daggers jab at it. "I was tired and planned to go to bed early. I got caught in a rainstorm without a coat and shivered through most of the day."

You continue the dreary and oft-repeated tale. "I accepted her invitation and thought, as I hung up the phone, how nice of her to ask me for dinner. Somebody cares whether I eat or starve. Then my rage began.

"I thought, 'I don't want to go. I don't feel well. I would rather stay home and eat a can of cold beans.' But I didn't have the guts to say no in the first place or to call her back and say I couldn't make it. Instead I got mad at myself."

You sniff a few times to clear your nose and ask cheerfully of the void behind, "Are you with me?"

You do not expect an answer so you keep going in the same breath, "By the time I met her I was in full fury, although keeping it to myself. I ate like a pig, figuring that was the only reason I was there, but didn't enjoy a mouthful. I might as well have been chewing charcoal sprinkled with sawdust and topped with cotton."

You are speechless with rage, thinking what a fool you are, both on and off the couch.

"You might look at how important food is to you," says the analyst, breaking what you feared would be another of those occasional ghastly fifty-minute silences.

"Of course food is important to me," you say indignantly. "If I didn't eat, I would starve to death."

"I didn't say you shouldn't eat," he says.

"Oh." You feel reassured. It is enough to starve for words around him without having to give up food, too.

"I merely suggest you look at how afraid you are of emptiness," he says.

"Emptiness!" you exclaim. "There's nothing worse."

"You certainly seem to abhor it," he agrees.

"Like nature abhors a vacuum, I abhor emptiness," you state. "It's the way we survive, fighting it. A child's stomach is empty, so he cries and gets food."

"I am not denying that," he says. "But it's hardly likely that you're going to starve to death."

"I sometimes feel I will," you say, "although I've heard of men who lived for days with little or no food; so I guess I could survive if I missed a meal or two."

You add ironically, "Especially if they're like the divine repast I endured last night. I caught my death of cold in that monsoon-ridden restaurant. Every time someone opened the door the winds roared in, hurricane-force."

"You certainly don't miss many meals in your dreams," he comments, still on the track of emptiness.

Your dreams are a glutton's delight, heaped high with the most fabulous of foods. Your fantasy banquet tables make Henry the Eighth look like a piker of the palate. Meats drown in fragrant sauces; vegetables float in butter. You create chocolate whipped-cream soufflés that rise as high as the Empire State Building on which sit white clouds of meringue sprinkled with flaky butterscotch.

"I'd never starve if I could eat my dreams," you assure him.

"You do eat them, in one sense, as you chew over your words about them here," he says.

"Sometimes they are more than I can swallow," you admit.

"But you do manage, in one way or another, to stuff yourself," he says. "Either with food or work or social activity or theories. If you do not have enough theories of your own, you race to the library to find books that will give you more."

"I'd look great lying here without a thought in my head," you say angrily.

"Why don't you try it?" he asks, and he is not being funny.

You are puzzled. "It never occurred to me that I could exist without thinking. I thought I always had to be figuring out what things mean."

"There was a time in your life when you didn't figure out anything," he says. "You just felt."

"Boy, if there was, it sure passed me by quickly," you quip.

"What do you think would happen if you stopped thinking?" he asks.

"I don't know," you say, "and I'm not sure I'd want to find out."

Then you add quickly, "I'd go crazy."

"Do you know that?" he asks. "Or is this another on-the-spot theory to fill emptiness so you won't have to feel things too acutely?"

"I'm damned if I know," you say, completely confused.

"Three cheers!" he exclaims.

"What for?" you ask in surprise.

"Because you said, 'I don't know,' instead of formulating some theory or jumping to some conclusion."

This is the weirdest session ever. It started out with your rage at giving in to an invitation to dine out. Now he praises you because you have admitted that you do not know something; whereas all the rest of your uncertain life if you confessed, "I don't know," you were made to feel ashamed and disgraced. It would bring you disapproving looks, punishment, and possible flunking in school, and later, when you went to work, would mark you as stupid and could even cost you your job.

But here you are being cheered for saying, "I don't know," as if you had just run fifty yards for a psychic touchdown.

"You mean I don't *have* to know?" you ask wistfully.

"Some things you will know; others you may never know or at least not be able to put into words," he says. "There's another kind of knowing besides formulating theories, unaccustomed as you are to it in later years."

"And you mean it's okay to feel empty?" You cannot quite believe it.

"I should think it's a relief to feel empty once in a while after the way you have stuffed yourself full of so many things," he says.

You know you have stuffed your life with work. You make sure you always have more than you can handle. The idea of spare time with nothing to do frightens you. You relish the frenzy of overwork, welcome the energy it consumes so that you will not have to worry about where to put it. The frantic pace may destroy you a few years earlier than you would otherwise die, but this is less hazardous than having time on your empty hands.

You make more dates than Elsa Maxwell, racing from one to the other, not enjoying most of them but preferring this to sitting at home tortured by loneliness. And when you are with people you fill the silences with endless, aimless chatter, words without meaning except to stave off emptiness.

You see too many movies, too many plays, read too many books, and look at too many television shows—all because you cannot bear doing nothing.

Yet it is all a farce because the empty feeling never disappears but merely gets covered up for a while. It always lurks underneath, ready to remind you of its poignant presence, the second you stand alone. You always thought you evaded it in sleep, but now you see that your dreams are stuffed with the emptiness of your life.

"What are you thinking?" the analyst asks.

"I am wondering what is so unbearable about emptiness." A thought strikes you. "Is that why you keep quiet so often? You want me to get acquainted with emptiness?"

"Don't you think that's a good idea?" he says.

You cannot honestly admit it is; but since most, if not all, of his ideas are good ones, you are loath to pass it by.

"Aren't my words another way for you to stuff yourself?" he asks. "When you feel empty, you demand that they flow forth to fill you up. But they do not satisfy the emptiness in you any more than you were satisfied last night with the dinner, which you did not enjoy because you were so raging mad."

"Why in hell was I so angry?" you ask of yourself, not him.

"Couldn't you just be in a rage, period?" he says. "Must you theorize about rage too?"

Yes, you must, at times, to your psychic detriment. You do not feel proud of the rage in which you have glimpsed yourself, looking backward from the couch. It is the rage of a clinging, possessive child who strangles his mother with insatiable demands—in children, understandable; but in someone your age, hardly admirable.

You now know that you did not suddenly become angry as an adult but have felt that way ever since childhood, for many, many reasons. When you were small you wondered, why do they do this to me, why do they say "Dirty baby, control your bladder," and "Little stinker, wipe your nose," and "Filthy child, don't touch yourself there"; and ever since then you felt disgusted with your once beautiful body, now a body horrible, which you make even more loathsome by afflicting it with strange diseases and ailments, as if to show everybody just how horrible you can be.

You are in a rage because of other things forgotten over the years but which unfurl in your dreams and the words that whirl out of dreams, a rage at the terrible closeness to your parents which you both desire and fight. You fight the closeness because it keeps you from moving gracefully and gaily away from them into a life of your own.

You raged at your parents for clutching at you, accusing them of living through you, using you to fill their—and you even thought of the very word long before the analyst spoke of it—emptiness.

But your own emptiness you had never accepted.

You were far too busy stuffing yourself full of whatever wonders the world around you offered—all the buzz-buzz of the busy people fleeing, as you were, from emptiness.

How often you sold your soul for a meal, as if the nourishment of food would appease the rage that simmered within. It was not food alone you sought, for those with whom you ate would stuff you in other ways, tell you how wonderful you were, show concern for what was happening to you.

And psychoanalysis was the final stuffing, another way to fill emptiness. But luckily a way that enabled you to understand your hunger, to know why you feared emptiness.

"Must I know what it is like to feel empty?" you ask him.

"It might help," he says.

Emptiness will not destroy you—what a delightful thought.

You inform him, "This is completely opposed to everything I have been taught, but I will try to understand that nothing terrible happens if I feel empty."

"It is time," he replies, and you think he is telling you that it is time you did so—but then you realize he is signifying that the hour is at an end.

You stand up and surprisingly enough, or rather, not surprisingly at all, your sore throat has disappeared, your nose has unstuffed itself, and you hold your head high as you walk out the door.

Sic gloria of the unconscious as it *transits* into the conscious.

I'm a Stranger Here Myself

One day as you lie on the couch a most revolutionary thought springs out of the depths of you freely, not forced out as formerly by frenzy.

The thought is: "*I* did it."

You did it. Nobody stood over you with gun or knife. You alone over the desperate years, willfully and unwillfully decided what to do, what to think, what to say.

In the days B.C. (Before Couch) you thought of yourself as a jellyfish, adrift on the shifting tides. But now you are a swift shark, attacking some of the wrong enemies perhaps, but fighting to keep alive.

You always believed yourself the innocent victim of life, target of the world's great fury, of the rage of its many men. You blamed everything outside yourself except the heavens, not quite willing to join those who clamp responsibility on the stars as they consult astrological charts to find out how they should live.

You blamed your parents for what went wrong with you, not seeing that you were the one who chose—in what you now know was purposeful design—exactly what you wished to use of their strengths, follies, and foibles. All impulses and fantasies were strictly your own.

An incident in your father's life helps you realize this. You are telling the analyst of the time your father, as a young man, ran away from home after a fight with his parents.

"I don't understand how he could have been a rebel," you say in amazement. "Both his parents were quiet, gentle people."

"Couldn't he have had some impulses of his own?" the analyst suggests.

Why of course, you think. And if your father had his own impulses, so did you. You were not a carbon copy of your parents. You possessed your own potentiality as a person. If you held your parents responsible for your unhappiness, then, indeed, you would doom yourself to misery, for that would be denying that you had any power at all, including the power to change.

For years you insisted, as though stamping your feet in a perpetual temper tantrum, that your parents be perfect, even though you would not, when you were little, and you would not now, exchange them for anybody else's parents.

Finally you have realized that it is enough your mother bore you. The struggle is yours from that day on.

You are able now to see your parents as human beings caught in their own torments, unable perhaps to pay as much attention to you as you craved in one way, perhaps more than they should have in another.

You can visualize your mother when you were born, a

young wife, eager to please your father, not too easy a man to please. Her mother had died when she was only three; and now that you understand what utter desolation a child feels when a mother leaves home even for a few hours, your heart goes out to your mother and what it meant to her to have had no mother during the truly tender years. She had less and less time for you after the birth of each successive child, but that did not mean she loved you the less—although to your angry soul it did of a certainty consign you to the role of Cinderella.

At the beginning of analysis it was as if the analyst talked to you about a stranger as he pointed out feelings in you that seemed foreign.

Often to yourself you denied what he said. "Who, me? He's got the wrong person."

Or you thought, "He's a nice guy but he's surely wrong about me sometimes."

To him you said courteously, "Do you really think so?" or, "Could it be?"

The stranger about whom he spoke was as distant a figure as the imaginary Man in the Moon, but you paid him the honor of listening, since you were paying him.

There comes a time, however, when you stop looking around the room for a mythical culprit, when you admit that perhaps it is your voice you have just heard speaking out in astounding revelation, and next time you must be more careful what you say—except that the longer you are in analysis, the less careful you get, fortunately for you.

Before you started analysis you thought you were an adult, but you can no longer deceive yourself about the angry child who screams away inside, mocking your attempts to be mature, destroying any chance for happiness. Only by accepting this angry child can you quiet his screams and appease the loneliness you have suffered over the years, which is the loneliness of those who feel deserted.

You now understand the appeal of Elvis Presley as he writhes uncontrolled and gyrating, like an angry child thrashing around the crib, pleading for somebody to love him.

You felt you had taken a beating in life, but you now know you gave yourself the beating. You drop the albatross of self-pity that has been draped in dead folds around your neck.

As you look at the people who whirled through your life, you realize that you selected those who voiced your anger and hunger. Everyone spoke for you but yourself; your only speaking was in the selection.

You were never attracted to the stable, serene souls, for they spoke in a key you could not hear. When the ones you chose, expecting them to be Fairy Godmothers or Prince Charmings, turned out instead to be wicked stepmothers or Bluebeards, you did not understand what had happened. You could not see that both they and you sought each other like trembling children in the night, searching solace from the nearest, warm human as protection against ogres. You did not understand that such a relationship holds the seeds of destruction from the start. It cannot survive because the demands that each makes on the other are the angry desires of years past which no one can fulfill, then or now, and which no one has a right to ask anyone else to fulfill.

You were never willing to take the blame for failure; but now that you know what happened, you can throw away the word "blame," another convenient word like the one with which it rhymes, "shame," to hide what you feel. Without blame, without shame, you accept the fact that you had created situations, again and again, which had a ring of familiarity, feeling at home in them even though they tortured you.

Consciously you may have wanted one thing, but unconsciously you desired something else even more—and you know now who wins in this struggle. The saying, "People do what they want to do," is true when it means "unconsciously want." You are surprised at nothing the unconscious achieves. Its ingenuity is beyond belief. It makes your conscious mind seem mediocre, helpless.

You say to the analyst, "Not only do people get the kind of government they deserve, but they also get the kind of people they deserve."

"What do you mean?" he asks. "Sometimes you are elliptical."

You are not quite sure what this word means, but you are pleased that you can puzzle him. You explain: "In the case of poor government, the people give no thought to the men they select or what those men stand for. It is the same with the choice of people in your life. When the selection is poor, it has been made strictly from hunger."

And then there are two strangers in the picture, yourself and the person you have chosen.

But now you are less of a stranger to yourself, thanks to the stranger who sits behind you, who will remain a stranger to the end, even though he comes closer to you, in one sense, than anyone ever has or will as he opens up a new way through life.

But he can only point out the way. He cannot force you to take it.

Yours alone is the decision whether to walk in that new direction or turn back to the old, painful path.

It is a decision made easier as you understand the lines from "The Rubáiyát of Omar Khayyám"—

And after many days my Soul return'd
And said, "Behold, Myself am Heav'n and Hell."

Of Myth and Magic

"I'm changing," you tell the analyst. "I feel it in my bones."

"That's where it counts," he says.

"This proves so many people wrong," you muse. "If I had a dime for every time I heard someone insist, 'You can't change human nature,' I would never have had to worry about paying for analysis."

You realize that those who aver that people cannot change are really saying, "*I* cannot change." They are welcome to speak for themselves—but not for *you.* Those who have never sought to change have no right to speak for those who seek to change.

"I feel as if I'm coming down, cloud by cloud, from Cloud Nine," you say. "I am descending like a feather, wafted back and forth by the winds of my resistance, but I'm earthbound at long last."

Then you ask thoughtfully, "Don't you think the only

chance the world has to survive is for everyone to be psychoanalyzed, from Arab to Zulu?"

"Good God, no!" he exclaims, sounding horrified.

"What?" You are equally horrified.

"Many people are not ready for it," he says. "They are too resistant to the truth."

Thinking about it, you grudgingly admit that perhaps not everyone is a qualified candidate for the couch. There are a number of souls, say 2,688,900,000 or so (current estimate places the world's population at 2,689,000,000) who would have no part of analysis even if enough analysts were available.

It has finally penetrated your no-longer-so-thick skull that you cannot persuade anyone by words or deeds to go into analysis. He has to be ready for change, want to change. You can lead someone to the couch but you cannot make him associate.

"There are a lot of fantasies about psychoanalysis, aren't there?" you ask.

"Why should it escape fantasies?" he says. "Nothing else does."

"I know people who believe it's a kind of magic," you say.

"So do I." He laughs. "Or rather, so did I. I don't think you believe that any longer."

"I've learned," you say. "But I have friends who have not been analyzed and seem to think that analysis can change black villains into white-robed crusaders. One of them says of each man with whom she falls in love, 'Oh, if he would only get analyzed, he'd make the perfect husband,' meaning he would become tender and thoughtful and propose to her."

"Analysis does not guarantee that people turn lovable

overnight," he says wryly. "Also, anyone who tries to send another into analysis runs the risk that during or after the analysis, the analyzed one may be attracted to someone else."

You bring up another fantasy. "Some think psychoanalysis is only for the very emotionally disturbed. They argue, 'You're not crazy, why do you need analysis?' "

"That's a distortion of the real facts," he says. "The very emotionally ill are the ones who take a long time to benefit by analysis. They can be helped but it is hard work and requires much patience on the part of the analyst."

"In other words, the more desperate you are, the harder it is for psychoanalysis to help," you say. "I can attest to that. As I felt less desperate I was able to move into my thoughts far more freely."

You add, "When I first came, it was like wading through water with the tide against me. Now I feel as if I am sailing with the current."

The high cost of analysis is another fantasy. When you go to an analyst, you are one of only seven to, say, fifteen patients he sees throughout the year, and each of his sessions runs fifty minutes. When you visit the average medical doctor, whose training is not as long or as specialized as the analyst's, you are likely to be one of 500 to 1000 patients he sees throughout the year and you see him for ten or fifteen minutes. You do not realize until you are in analysis how much time you take up.

"There's another fantasy in the minds of those who chide me for going into analysis or remaining in it what they think is a long time," you say to the analyst. "They call it a crutch."

"These people are unable to see the crutches with which they stagger around, crutches they will never be able to throw away and on which they will lean even more desperately in time," he says. "If analysis is a temporary crutch, at least it aims to strengthen you so that you can walk alone."

"The unbelievers do not have to understand why I started or why I stay in or what I get out of it," you say. "It is not important they do. They live the way they think best and I should be accorded the same privilege."

You realize that your faith in the analytic process is now so strong you do not need to defend it so violently. You know that its angriest defenders may be among the weakest believers.

"Psychoanalysis is doing very well without the support of the snipers," says the analyst.

"It certainly is," you agree. "Just think. Fifty years ago only eight men believed in it, while the rest of the world scorned it. Today the world holds several thousand psychoanalysts, and millions of people accept psychoanalysis as the way to truth."

"You can't fool the unconscious," he says. "Not in the long run."

You mention still another fantasy about analysis. "Sometimes you hear a person say, 'Oh, I was psychoanalyzed and it didn't help a bit.' It turns out that he visited a marriage counselor several times or saw an analyst for consultation and this, to him, is psychoanalysis."

"There are also those who remain in it for a short while and then stop for one reason or another," he says. "You cannot call that psychoanalysis either."

"What about the demand that psychoanalysis provide some sort of statistical proof of its success?" you ask.

"That's ridiculous to anyone who believes in psychoanalysis," he says. "It's impossible to compile statistics about analysis. Freud pointed out that the uniformity which forms a basis for statistics is lacking. He said it would be like adding apples, pears, and nuts. You can't, because they are three different things."

You bring up another myth. "One of the country's most gifted novelists told me he had a horror of being analyzed because it would destroy his creativity. I've heard this fantasy expressed many times."

"Analysis destroys nothing except inner chaos and the darkness of doubt," he says. "It clears away the cobwebs of childhood fantasies and often allows the creative capacity that exists, be it for painting or writing or designing skyscrapers, to come through more easily. Analysis does not give you talent if you do not possess it, any more than it takes away talent if you have it."

Since beginning analysis you find that you work far more easily. There are moments immediately after sessions when you cannot work at all, but they do not last. When you work there is a feeling of freedom that you never experienced before.

You conclude that people are creative in spite of their unhappiness, not because of it. One of your friends is able to put his fantasies to work in his painting. Another, unable to harness his desire to write, spends his days deep in fantasy, feeling bereft of talent and energy. One is able to use his fantasies to enrich himself and the world, and possesses a strength lacking in the one who allows his fantasies to drive him far from reality.

You recall a major-league baseball player who started to suffer from a strange obsession. At certain times in the game he became unable to move from the small spot in the field that was his regular position. A friend who had been psychoanalyzed suggested to the player that he go to an analyst for help.

As he lay on the couch talking, he discovered that he was unable to move only after he had missed catching a ball or after he struck out. He also recalled that when he was a boy, his father would lock him in a closet to punish him when he had misbehaved.

His inability to move was the unconscious re-enactment of the punishment he felt he deserved when he made an error or failed to hit. The small space on the field to which he became rooted, in which he symbolically locked himself, was, to his unconscious, the closet of boyhood days. When he understood this, and also came to feel it was natural for him to strike out occasionally or miss a fly, he lost the need to stand rooted.

The analysis did not affect his basic capacity as a ball player. It removed the obstacle in the way of his becoming as good as he was potentially, and, more important, a player who enjoyed the game rather than suffered through it.

You wonder how many men of skill endure similar punishments inflicted on themselves, not quite so dramatically, but which keep them from full and rich achievements.

You raise a final fantasy about psychoanalysis. "Some believe psychoanalysis is opposed to religion. How do you feel about it?"

"They are two very different things and do not have to be set up against each other like opponents in a chess game," he replies.

As you think about this answer, you realize how true it is. The rituals of religion offer solace and safety, and their power is not to be denied. There is a serenity you feel in church, listening to the richness of the organ, gazing at the beauty of stained glass, awed by the thousands of years of man's faith symbolized by the altar.

There is another serenity you get from psychoanalysis, a serenity that needs no music, no beauty of color, no reminder of the faith of other men down through the ages.

It is a serenity that stems from your soul alone. It comes out of wisdom born of pain and patience and the belief that the noblest struggle of all is to "know thyself."

Epilogue

"Would I like psychoanalyis?" asks a friend.

"I'm not sure you're expected to like it," you say.

"If you don't like it, why go into it?" asks the friend.

"Because the greater burden is not to know what you feel."

"Did you find out what you feel?"

"I think I know the depth of my anger," you reply. You recall the time you argued with the analyst that fear caused anger and he said perhaps it was the other way around. Now you know it does not make any difference which comes first because when you can accept anger, the fear disappears.

"I don't understand how you kept going so long. Weren't you all talked out months ago?" asks the friend.

"It takes quite a while to know the secret part of yourself," you explain. "At first you spend hours fighting against knowledge of it. Then, as you start to explore it, you find vast depths."

"What has analysis done for you?" the friend asks.

"It's given me the chance to be more the person I would like to be."

"You're not perfect by any means," the friend assures you.

"If I still expected to be perfect, it would mean that I needed more analysis," you reply.

"If you'll pardon me for saying so, I think it's a waste of time," says the friend. "Life is cruel and you might as well accept it as such."

"It is not the cruelty of life that troubles us but our impulses to be cruel. The answer is to be aware of these impulses so they do not hurt you or others."

"You make it sound so complicated," says the friend with a frown. "Life is a very simple thing."

Simpletons would have it so, you think; but instead you say, "Life is not a simple thing. Growing up and becoming civilized is not simple at all."

"The answers are all in the books," says the friend loftily.

"No book has the answer to important questions," you say, "because there are no answers outside yourself. You have to face the fantasies that have haunted you over the years."

"You spent your money for *that?*" the friend asks incredulously.

"It's worth far more than I could ever pay to clear away the fog of fraudulent fantasies through which I staggered all my life."

"What's the percentage?" asks the friend.

"Anger carries its own dreadful punishment. What you

desire in angry fantasy is bound to boomerang, pinning you to the cross of guilt."

"I thought the days of crucifying people were over," says the friend sarcastically.

"Not self-crucifixion. You drive in the spikes of suffering with your own furious hands."

"Why would anyone want to suffer?" asks the friend in wonder.

"You don't want to consciously, but you suffer because you still scream, 'Take care of me.' You pay a truly terrible price for this prison of dependence to which you sentence yourself."

"I don't think *I'm* dependent," says the friend.

"Only you know that," you answer. "Analysis has taught me it's impossible to know what lies inside anyone else. It's all I can do to understand myself. I would not presume to speak for you."

"Not even to tell me how to be happy?" asks the friend in wistful voice.

"No one can tell anyone else how to be happy. Each one has to find his own way." You try not to sound oracular, even though the friend asks for it.

"Are you happy?" the friend asks abruptly.

"Happier than I ever have been. I wish I might have lived part of my life differently, but I understand now why I did what I did and am able to forgive myself."

"I will admit you don't rush around like crazy any more," says the friend. "But I hardly think *that's* worth a psychoanalysis."

You recall the hours of tears. The struggle to unleash inner furies. The relentless search for truth and the slow acceptance of it. The facing of fantasies that fashioned the urgency, making so much of your life a meaningless test of strength.

But all you can think of in reply to your friend is a passage from *Alice in Wonderland.* You say, "Wait a minute. I want to get something that puts it better than I could."

You haul out Lewis Carroll's classic and read:

> "The game's going on rather better now," she said by way of keeping up the conversation a little.
>
> " 'Tis so," said the Duchess; "and the moral of that is—'Oh, 'tis love, 'tis love, that makes the world go round!' "
>
> "Somebody said," Alice whispered, "that it's done by everybody minding their own business!"
>
> "Ah, well! It means much the same thing," said the Duchess, digging her sharp little chin into Alice's shoulder as she added, "and the moral of *that* is—'Take care of the sense, and the sounds will take care of themselves.' "

You close the book.

Your friend looks at you, puzzled. "And pray, what is the moral of *that?*"

"The moral might be that if everybody minded his own business, that is to say, minded knowing himself, the world would go round in love, not anger."

You add, "Or perhaps the moral might be that if we take care of the non-sense, the sounds will take care of themselves."

"Meaning the sounds of fury inside us?" asks the friend.

You nod, happy he has understood. To yourself you

think that really the only moral is that there is no moral at all.

For, as you looked within, you discovered that all the pious, philosophical platitudes served but to hide truth. There is only the self, and everybody's self is different from all others and must be respected for that difference. Thus, the true dignity of man.

Catalog